The Birdkeepers' Guide

AFRICAN GREYS

The Birdkeepers' Guide

AFRICAN GREYS

GREG GLENDELL

T.F.H. Publications, Inc.

Published by
T.F.H. Publications, Inc.
One TFH Plaza
Third and Union Avenues
Neptune City, NJ 07753

ISBN 978-0-7938-0652-6

Printed and Bound in China
05 06 07 08 09 1 3 5 7 9 8 6 4 2

Library of Congress Cataloging-in-Publication Data
Glendell, Greg.
  Birdkeepers' guide to African greys / Greg Glendell.
      p. cm.
  Includes index.
  ISBN 978-0-7938-0652-2 (alk. paper)
  1. African gray parrot. I. Title.
SF473.P3G545 2008
636.6'865—dc22
                          2007035808

The Leader In Responsible Animal Care For Over 50 Years!®
www.tfh.com

CENTRAL
Garden & Pet

Greg Glendell BSc (Hons)

Greg Glendell has had a lifelong interest in birds. As an amateur ornithologist he has carried out fieldwork on bird habitat requirements and the breeding biology of native British birds. Following his degree in Environmental Science, which included coursework on animal and human behavior, he worked in wildlife conservation. He acquired his first parrot, a blue-fronted Amazon, in 1986 and this led to him developing a deep interest in these birds. He has bred parrots but no longer does so as there is a surplus of these birds in need of good homes. He keeps several parrots including greys, Amazons, and a Meyer's. Greg works as the UK's only full-time pet parrot behavioral consultant and is based in Somerset. You can e-mail Greg at mail@greg-parrots.co.uk and visit his website: www.greg-parrots.co.uk <http://www.greg-parrots.co.uk/> for more details of his consultancy. He is the author of *Breaking Bad Habits in Parrots* (2007).

Acknowledgements

Greg would like to thank Rachel Lewis for her comments on the text. Red, Sidney, Jasper and Doris performed to their usual high standards.

CONTENTS

CHAPTER 1

Origins of the grey parrot

There are two types of grey parrot kept as pet birds; the more common African grey, sometimes called the 'Congo' African grey and the smaller Timneh grey. 'Timneh' refers to the West African islands which are part of this bird's range. Although grey parrots come from West African countries, most 'pet' birds are now bred in captivity. These birds are well-known for their remarkable abilities to mimic sounds including replicating human speech.

Are the two types separate species?

The two types of grey are currently said to be closely related to each as other as subspecies. But this may change, and they may soon be considered as separate species. When seen together, they are quite distinct from one another. The African grey is nearly a third bigger than the Timneh being around 13in (33cm) in length. All adult African greys have a vivid red tail; immature birds' tails are also red, but with a dull brownish band near the tip. The beak is all black. An immature bird's eyes are dark when only a few weeks old, but this turns to pale grey and finally a straw-coloured yellow by the time the bird is a year old. The smaller Timneh is about 10in (25cm) in length, usually a darker grey, but the tail is always a very dark red, almost black color. The Timneh's beak is mainly black but it has a pale horn-coloured patch on the top bill. Like the African grey, the Timneh's eyes change colour during their first year of life. They start out very dark, changing to pale grey, finally becoming yellow in the adult, but this is a slightly paler, sometimes greenish-yellow compared with the adult African grey's straw-coloured eyes.

The natural habitat of grey parrots is lowland tropical rainforest. The population of the Timneh grey is much smaller than that of the African grey and the Timneh is found to the western end of the bird's complete range. They can be found throughout their range in dense forest or at the edges of the forest close to farmed land where they may feed on farmed crops. The birds are secretive in their habits and difficult to see except when flying overhead between feeding and roosting sites.

Timneh

African grey

⇧ **Timneh greys are found** *from Guinea Bissau east to the Ivory Coast. African greys range from the Ivory Coast east to Kenya.*
African greys are the ⇨ **largest** *parrot in central Africa.*

⇧ **The African grey's vivid red** *tail distinguishes it from the Timneh grey.*

How greys live in the wild

Greys are highly social birds. In the wild, they are always found in the company of their own kind, either living as a flock (which can number many hundreds of birds) or as pairs of birds in their forest habitat. As they wake up each morning, the birds will get ready to set off in search of food found elsewhere in the forest. At this time the birds call to each other with a repertoire of whistles, squawks, and harsh screeching noises. Soon they leave their roosting site and fly to the first feeding sites which may be many kilometres away. As with many other birds, when watching the flock, you can clearly see that most birds fly as pairs, with the same two birds staying close to each other during flight and when landing. Other greys that are breeding in the area will join this flock and feed communally for much of the daytime, often flying great distances between feeding sites. Grey parrots fly fast at around 40mph (65kph) so they can cover many hundreds of miles each week as they search out their favorite foods throughout their habitat.

Greys eat a wide range of foods

Their main sources of food are the fruits, nuts, flowers, leaves, and seeds they find on a range of forest trees, including palm trees. When feeding in the trees, they use their strong feet, aided by their equally strong beak as an extra 'hand' to climb amongst the branches as they feed. They have a range of techniques for dealing with different foods. Seeds and small nuts are easily cracked open with their powerful crushing beak and larger nuts and fruits can be held in one foot as they use their beak to get at the most nutritious parts. Tender shoots and leaves form part of their diet, and they can easily climb out to reach these on the tips of the tree branches. Soft fruit is also eaten, sometimes by the bird mashing up the fruit pulp with its beak and just drinking up the juice. The birds also come down to the ground occasionally to feed on certain plants, which ensures they obtain their essential minerals, including calcium. In addition to this, they also eat small quantities of soil, which is believed to aid their digestion.

⇧ **Wild greys come down** *to the ground for some food, but they are very nervous when doing so.*

Greys are expert climbers *and can reach the* ⇨ *tender shoots and leaves at the end of a branch.*

⇩ **The grey's habitat is under threat**
from logging in many countries.

⇧ **Greys rely on a range of tropical**
rainforest trees for their food and as
secure nesting sites.

How greys live in the wild

When the feeding flock includes breeding birds, these will leave and later rejoin the flock as necessary because they have to make regular trips back to their nests. But the flock as a whole may stay together throughout the day. In the afternoon, the birds have a quiet 'siesta' period for an hour or two when they doze and preen, avoiding other activities in the heat of the day. Later in the afternoon and early evening, they start feeding again. Following these feeding activities, they return to their roosting site, occasionally flying while it is almost dark. On most days in tropical Africa, it rains and the rain can come down in very heavy showers, so everything, including the

⇦ **Wild greys get drenched** *every day, and pet birds need to be sprayed to maintain feather condition.*

birds gets completely drenched. The parrots actually seem to enjoy this. They will roll around in the trees as it rains trying to get the feathers wet as they open their wings to catch the rain. These daily showers are vital to help them keep their feathers in good condition. After the rain, they spend much time shaking the excess water off, preening and tidying up their feathers.

Coming from an equatorial area, there is little change in daylight length throughout the year and the birds get equal amounts (about 12 hours) of darkness and daylight each day. Greys are playful birds and indulge in mock fights and occasionally tease each other as they clamber through the trees. They live in a habitat where food is quite plentiful, and although they will spend many hours feeding and flying between feeding sites, non-breeding birds do have quite a bit of free time to play and enjoy themselves.

The language of greys

Greys are highly intelligent creatures and they have a large repertoire of calls and postures which they use as their language. By these means, they can show the other members of their flock how they are reacting to things going on around them and what action to take on seeing a predator. Like most parrots, greys are highly vulnerable to predation and potential threats include hawks, mammals (including humans), and reptiles. They have a range of calls that they use depending on the nature of the threat and the proposed action to take. The flock may have to make rapid decisions about whether to flee from a hawk or just hide from the danger within the trees as the predator passes by. In their own way, the birds know that their lives depend on them being attuned to everything going on around them and they are by nature very wary birds. Greys in captivity have, of course, retained this nervous disposition.

While the natural repertoire of calls *is very* ⇨ *similar between Timneh greys and African greys, there are some differences between the two types.*

⇧ **Some greys within a flock** *act as sentinel birds and keep a watch for any threats.*

Greys naturally spend ⇨
some time *keeping
their feathers in good
condition by
participating in regular
preening sessions.*

The meaning of body language

Alone grey parrot, lost and out of contact with its flock, is much more vulnerable to being taken by a predator. Living in a flock gives each bird a degree of protection it would not otherwise have, as each bird is always on the lookout for dangers and ready to tell the whole flock of any threat to their safety. But the pair bond between adult breeding birds is also very strong. In addition to the loud screeches and screams used to communicate over some distances to flock members, the birds also have a repertoire of much softer calls which they use to communicate with their partner or, as young birds, with their siblings. They also have a system of raising certain feathers, particularly facial feathers as part of their "body language." Birds can tell if each appears alert, or relaxed, or frightened, or playful. Greys often ask their mate to preen their head. Here, one bird raises its head feathers and keeps its eyes sunken in or half-closed as it offers its head to be preened. Such mutual preening certainly strengthens the pair bond between adult birds, but it also takes place between siblings. Usually, after one bird has preened the other for a few seconds, they swap roles and so each bird gets preened.

Minimal aggression
While aggressive encounters tend to be rare, birds will give plenty of warning before actually fighting. When giving a warning, a grey will fluff up most of its body feathers and make a sharp mechanical clicking sound once or twice by snapping its lower bill against the upper bill. Like most parrots, greys have voluntary control of their iris and pupil and a display of aggression often includes contracting their iris or "pinning" their eyes as it is also called. Generally at this stage, one bird will back down readily to avoid further conflict.

Parrots under pressure
The daily life of grey parrots is certainly a busy one. They live by being sensitive to their surroundings and are very cautious in their behaviors. As their forest habitat is now being reduced through logging for the timber trade, they are under more pressure to find alternative sources of food, and this can include agricultural crops. Due to these feeding habits, some birds are seen as pests in agricultural areas on the edges of the forest.

This bird is 'pinning' his ⇧ eyes: *this is a clear sign that he is very excited about something.*

⇩ A very relaxed grey. *The head feathers form a little 'ruff' around the back of the head and the cheek feathers are raised.*

⇧ This grey is alert *and attentive. The raised feathers around the cheeks show that the bird is in a relaxed mood.*

⇩ This grey asks his mate, *a Timneh, for a head scratch; note the sunken, relaxed eye and the way in which the bird on the right presents his head and neck to be preened.*

Breeding in the wild

Grey parrots use holes in trees for their nests. Generally these are existing holes, high up in the trunk of a tree. Often, an existing hole is enlarged, and the birds are easily capable of excavating these using their powerful beaks. They also use their feet to help enlarge the hole. The birds do not carry any material to the nesting hole; the eggs, two to four, are laid on the wood chippings of the floor of the hole. The female takes on most of the responsibility for incubation and caring for the chicks, but males do help as well. The male will return regularly to feed his mate on regurgitated food, which he stores in his crop. This is vital for the female when she is incubating the eggs and brooding the very young chicks.

Chicks call before hatching

After about 25 days' incubation, the chicks start to call from within the egg, and they begin to establish their contact calls with their parents. The eggs will then hatch two or three days later. The chicks emerge blind and partially covered in grey down feathers. At this age they are completely dependent on their parents for all their needs. The parents feed the chicks on partially digested regurgitated food and the babies develop quite rapidly. Usually they are ready to take their first flight and leave the nest (to fledge) by about 13 weeks of age. At this age the young birds are extremely naïve. They are very vulnerable to attacks from predators and still incapable of feeding themselves.

While the urge to fly is very strong in the birds at this age, their first few flights are clumsy, as the skills of flying can only be developed by trial and error. The young birds will stay with their parents for many months as they learn which things to eat, what to avoid, and how to take the appropriate action at the sight of predators or threats. The process of becoming independent of their parents is a long one and these youngsters remain highly reliant on their parents and other flock members for their own safety for up to a year. Many recently fledged birds fail to survive, but those who learn fast, remain alert at all times, and develop their flying skills rapidly stand a good chance of surviving. At three or four years of age they are sexually mature and will begin attempts to breed, but this depends on finding a suitable nesting hole.

⇧ **These recently fledged** *captive-bred Timneh grey siblings play together.*

⇩ **The chicks on the left** *are about two weeks old. At six weeks (center) their first true feathers are growing through. After eight weeks (right) they lose most of their down feathers.*

Note the dark, almost black, eye *of this very young African grey. When the bird is five months old, the eyes turn pale grey, later still becoming straw-yellow.* ⇨

CHAPTER 2

Greys as companion birds

Grey parrots are popular as pet birds partly because of their well-known abilities as mimics. However enticing the idea of a parrot with a good talking ability is, this should not be the main reason for acquiring one of these birds. As with other parrots, greys—even captive-bred ones—are not domesticated creatures and they retain all their wild-type behavioral needs and repertoire. The life of a grey parrot in the wild is very different from the life we ask them to lead in captivity. The key to keeping greys well as pets is to enable them to carry out as many of their wild-type behaviors in captivity as possible. Unless they are kept by owners who understand these needs, problems—particularly behavioral problems—may soon crop up.

Greys are high maintenance pets

In general greys are, almost by default, nervous, even suspicious, birds. This stems simply from the fact that as a species they are highly vulnerable to being preyed upon by a variety of other creatures, including humans. It is literally in their genes to be very cautious about things going on around them, and they are often suspicious of seemingly harmless objects or actions. If this aspect of their disposition is not understood, grey parrots can become very fearful birds, even becoming afraid of their main caregiver. They easily recognise people as different individuals. Just because a grey likes one person does not mean that someone else can (or should) handle it.

They are also very intelligent, and in captivity they need to be kept occupied with a range of tasks. This can include playing with a variety of toys and, most importantly, not being kept for long periods in a cage or in its aviary every day. For the sake of the bird's mental and physical well-being, it will need to be out of the cage with you for many hours each day, so a grey parrot is not an easy maintenance pet. Once they are no longer immature (at around two to three years old), some greys are inclined to become one-person birds, and they may reject having anything to do with anyone else, other than their favored person. The tendency for this to occur can be reduced by suitable training, as discussed later.

⬅ **Greys raise and stretch their wings** as a greeting gesture, as though saying "Hello." This is usually seen when they recognise another bird or person already known to them.

This plastic ball and bell makes a sound when played with.

⬅ **Try to get your bird** used to a carrying cage, which you'll need for future transport.

⬆ **Toys in the bird's cage** should be changed from time to time, and swapped for new or different ones, so the bird does not get bored with having the same items to play with all the time.

Behavioral characteristics

Although African greys and Timneh greys seem very similar to one another, many people who have kept both types do identify significant differences between them as companion birds. Timnehs tend to be a little more confident than African greys. Because African greys are more nervous, they are also more inclined to pluck their feathers when they are under stress or bored. Since Timnehs seem to be a little more easy-going, they are also less likely to become one-person birds.

However, the factor that causes much bigger differences between individual birds' qualities as companion birds is how they were raised. While some wild-caught imported birds may still be sold as pet birds, they remain so nervous of people that they rarely adjust well to life as a pet bird. For this reason, most grey parrots produced for the pet trade are now captive-bred. Captive-bred birds may be hand-reared, parent-reared, or part-parent reared, and major differences in the behavior of these birds when they mature can be caused by the methods used to raise them. Birds that have never seen their own parents and were hand-reared from the day they hatched from the egg can present special problems as adult parrots. These birds often become overdependent on one person and they seem more prone to behavioral problems such as plucking. Having missed out on the normal interactions with their own parents, they don't see themselves as parrots, but identify purely with humans for all their needs. They often lack confidence in new situations. These birds are much easier to sell since they show submissive behaviors and are described as "cuddle tame" when on sale as babies.

Parent-raised birds are best

Conversely parent-raised greys are less tame as babies, but develop into normal adults and are less likely to experience behavioral problems. They also have more confidence and a degree of independence which renders them less prone to overbonding with one person. Part-parent raised birds are those which have been raised by their parents for a few weeks, at least until their eyes have opened, but where the process has been completed by hand-rearing. The behavior of these birds as adults falls somewhere between the other two types and they can do quite well as pet birds. Hand-reared birds are far more commonly available than parent- or part-parent raised birds. However, if you can obtain a parent- or part-parent raised bird, these usually make better companion birds.

Grey parrots as companion birds

Eye is more yellow in African grey.

Timnehs are usually darker on the back and wings than African greys.

African Grey

The Timneh's eye is sometimes more greenish than the African grey's.

A Timneh's top bill is always pale horn-coloured on the front.

Timnehs are about one-third smaller than African greys.

Timneh

The African grey's tail is much brighter red in colour.

⇧ **The most obvious differences** between the two greys are the greater size of the African grey and this bird's vivid red tail. The smaller Timneh has a duller, maroon-red tail.

⇦ **These birds (far left)** were raised for the first six weeks by their own parents; then hand-reared (left). Their prospects are better than any bird who is hand-reared and fed by syringe from day one.

Intelligence and sensitivity

While all parrots are very intelligent birds, most scientific work on parrot intelligence has been done on grey parrots. Greys can be taught to use human language in its proper context and can name hundreds of objects and make requests to be given specific ones. They can name and classify hundreds of objects with

⇧ **Irene Pepperberg** tests one of her grey parrots, Alex, on his knowledge of colors and shapes.

regards to their color, shape and sizes. Greys can also count (up to six!).

Compared with other parrots, such as Amazons, macaws, cockatoos and conures, grey parrots are usually less noisy and can be rather shy, almost introverted, birds. They tend to be very wary of new things, including new people, new toys, or a change in their diet. Where this characteristic is seen in pet birds, it is partly due to the fact that the bird is removed from its

normal way of living, which would be within a flock of birds. Greys living in groups are much more confident birds than those who have to live on their own. Like other parrots, greys should not be thought of as easy-maintenance pets who can spend all day in a cage. Deprived of the freedom of spending many hours each day out of their cage in the company of their caregivers, these birds become bored, and the stress of boredom can cause them to show behavioral problems. Greys are very inclined to pick at their own feathers if any aspect of their care is neglected.

A calm household is needed

As highly intelligent birds, they need a lot of stimulation. The caregiver must ensure that the bird can be kept interested in things, that it has access to a range of toys which are changed around regularly, and that the type of household they are to live in is suitable for such a sensitive bird. Grey parrots do not do well in a house which is too busy with boisterous children or dogs or other pets running around. This would make the bird even more nervous and possibly fearful. Greys need to be with a family where the general atmosphere is calm and stable. This allows their confidence to grow and over time the depth of their character will become apparent. Most importantly, before considering

◁ **This hand-reared grey** has bitten off some of his own feathers.

⇧ *Greys are intelligent and complex* birds and require much commitment from their owners if they are to do well as companion birds. They have a similar life expectancy to humans.

⇦ *Once a bird trusts you,* he will love having his head scratched gently like this for brief periods. This is very comforting for them.

getting a grey, you need to be sure you really do have the time to care for such a demanding and sensitive creature. Greys are not easy birds to keep well as companion animals.

Acquiring a grey

There are many different places where you can obtain a grey parrot. While pet shops and some garden centers might seem the most obvious sources, you can also check listings in birdkeeping magazines. Private advertisements appear in local papers, often with older birds being offered. While some businesses advertise birds on the Internet, you should make sure you visit the seller and see the bird in its current home and reassure yourself that you trust the seller before acquiring the bird. Also, make sure you have some form of guarantee as to the bird's health before parting with your money and get a detailed receipt for your bird which includes date of purchase and species of bird.

Adopting a parrot

As with some other pets, there are actually far more parrots in need of good homes than there are good homes available for them. Many birds end up in rescue centers and sanctuaries. Some of these places do foster their birds out to suitable homes. In most cases, you will be adopting, rather than taking ownership of the bird, provided the sanctuary feels you can provide the right type of home. Some parrots from these places may have behavioral problems, and this may be the reason why they were given to a sanctuary in the first place. But in the circumstances where an older bird has always been a pet bird, you may be able to offer it better one-to-one attention than staff at a sanctuary are able to provide. To find details of these sources you can search the Internet using the words 'parrot sanctuary' or 'parrot rescue' or 'parrot re-homing,' etc. Or you could contact the ASPCA (RSPCA in the UK) and ask them for details of bona fide sources of birds in need of good homes.

Birds are sometimes described as being tame but later prove not to be. If a bird is advertised as tame, make sure you see the seller handling the bird and observe if the bird is comfortable with being handled, even if this is only coming onto the hand. In the world of birdkeeping, it is a case of "Let the buyer beware," so take your time when selecting a bird from the range of sources available.

⇧ **If a bird on sale in a pet shop** like this is offered to the purchaser as "tame," make sure that this is the case before considering buying it. Ask to see it being handled as proof of the claim.

⇦ **This young grey** has been badly wing-clipped. Take care when buying a clipped bird, for some are more nervous than normal.

⇧ **Plenty of websites advertise** birds for sale but do not acquire a bird without actually first going to see it and meeting the seller.

Recognizing a healthy bird

Like may birds, greys tend to hide any signs of being unwell and try to appear normal. They can do this right up to the point at which they are seriously ill, so you need to be able to recognize a healthy bird by looking for the tell-tale signs. Healthy birds are active for most, but not all, of the daytimc. The eyes should be bright and wide open. There should be no discharge from the nostrils and the breathing should be silent. The bird should be alert and well aware of things going on around it. The body feathers should be in good condition. They should not be fluffed up but slightly smoothed down. The bird should be eating normally and passing droppings normally, without undue straining. The area around the vent should be clean, not soiled by droppings. When at rest or sleeping, a healthy bird usually stands on one foot.

Some birds that are sold as immature and "cuddly tame," usually from a pet shop, do not reveal the true character that they will display when adult. Immature birds tend to show submissive behaviours to everyone. Consequently, there is an advantage in getting an older bird (generally from a private sale) as the bird's true character will be well-formed and there are unlikely to be any major changes to this. While older birds are often sold for genuine reasons, many are also sold because their owners are experiencing problems with the bird with which they cannot cope. The most common of these are high noise levels, nervousness, and aggression, so ask about these aspects of the bird's character as well. Often these behavioral problems are not difficult to address, as discussed later (see pages 80-85).

Consult an avian vet

Birds that are unwell will show the opposite of these signs: fluffed-up feathers, an inattentive disposition, sleepy with dull, perhaps half-closed, eyes. When you see a bird that does not show the normal healthy signs, something may be wrong, so take care if you are considering purchase of such a bird. You can always ask the owner to have the bird checked by a specialist avian vet before you buy it and see the vet's report. Failing this, it is certainly worth having a vet check done within a day or two of acquiring the bird.

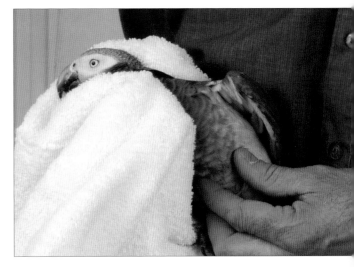

Grey parrots as companion birds

Clear nostrils, silent breathing, eyes bright and alert.

Dull, sunken eye.

The feathers are relaxed, not held down overly tightly.

This bird's body and head feathers are fluffed up and she is resting on both feet.

⇧ **Unhealthy bird.** This bird shows some signs of not being well. She appears inattentive and tired. Further checks on her condition should be made to assess her overall health accurately.

⇧ **Healthy bird.** This healthy grey is in good condition, with a bright alert eye and clear nostrils.

⇦ **A specialist bird vet (far left)** can examine a bird in more detail; this bird is having its chest muscles felt to determine its general health and muscle condition. Healthy birds usually sleep on one foot **(left)** and hold the other up under their feathers.

CHAPTER 3

The sense of sight

As with other parrots, a grey's keenest sense is its sight and these birds have a number of adaptations to their eyes which greatly improve their vision compared to human sight. The part of the eye you can see is only a small part of the eyeball itself, which is much larger. Examination of the skull of a bird and its eye-sockets reveals the true size of the eyeballs. Parrot's eyes are arranged to give them almost 360-degree, all-round vision, both vertically and horizontally. This ensures they can easily spot danger which may come from any direction. They also have good binocular (stereo) vision, as we do, for objects which are near and in front of them. All parrots can switch back and forth between their all-round monocular vision to close-up stereo vision in a split second.

Better color vision than humans

Parrots' eyes are somewhat flattened, not spherical like ours, so they have limited eye-movement within the socket. Instead, they tend to move the whole head when looking at objects. Parrots also have a third eyelid which you can see as a pale membrane when the bird blinks. While human color vision is limited to mixes of red, green and blue light, parrots see ultraviolet light as another one or two distinct colors as well. This is thought to help them distinguish between the sexes, as some color differences between males and females may only occur in UV colors. Such vision may also help them to identify the fruits they commonly eat from some distance and determine which of these are ripe. Unlike humans, parrots have voluntary control of their iris, and can open and close their pupils rapidly at will. This ability to "flash" their eyes is used to express excitement or to threaten another bird.

Birds process visual information at a much higher rate than we do. Our brain takes in about 16 images per second from our eyes. Films and videos are projected at around 25 frames per second, so this gives humans the illusion of a moving image. However, birds can take in 70 to 170 images per second. They probably need to be able to do this in order to see well when flying at high speed through the trees.

⇧ **The position of a grey's eyes** give it almost complete all-round vision vertically and horizontally.

⇧ **As this bird blinks (above),** its third eyelid which extends as a pale membrane over the surface of the eye becomes visible. A nervous or frightened bird shows a wide staring eye **(above right)** which is fully opened.

⇩ **Cross-section through a parrot's eye.** The vascular pecten, unique to birds, is thought to assist with blood circulation within the eye.

Parrots can turn their heads 180 degrees on each side to ensure good vision.

⇦ **On seeing any signs of danger,** the bird will sound an alarm note appropriate to the nature of the threat.

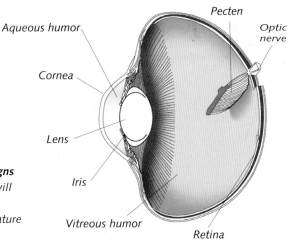

Aqueous humor

Cornea

Lens

Iris

Vitreous humor

Pecten

Optic nerve

Retina

Hearing, touch, temperature and

There is no external ear on a bird, but the opening to the ears lies just below and behind the eyes. The feathers covering the ear are sparse and allow sound waves to pass through easily. A parrot's ears work in much the same way as our ears; they are used not only to hear a similar range of sounds, but to detect gravity, ensure balance, and maintain appropriate body position. Vibrations of air caused by sound pass down the open ear tube to the eardrum. Here, these vibrations are passed through a tiny bone to the inner fluid-filled ear, which relays signals to the brain. Grey parrots hear a similar range of sounds to humans; and certainly produce sounds in a similar range.

Position of ear

Keeping a level head!

Parrots have an arrangement of three fluid-filled semicircular canals in the inner ear for ensuring both balance and maintenance of the correct attitude of the body during flight. Despite the banking, diving, and rolling movements birds

⇧ **Grey's feet are very sensitive** to touch and to vibrations on the perch. Even in darkness, the bird can tell from which side any disturbance is coming.

use in flight, they tend to keep their heads as level as possible at all times while flying.

The whole of a bird's body is sensitive to touch through the skin. This includes disturbance to feathers, light touching, and pain. Two areas are particularly sensitive to touch for parrots; the tongue and the feet. Parrots are perhaps unique amongst birds in the way they use their tongue. The first contact with some new food or object is normally via the front of the beak which is used to prod it, perhaps to see if it is safe. Then the tongue is used much like a finger-tip to feel it. All parrots' tongues are very muscular, as well as sensitive to temperature and texture. They are used to find the weakest point in nuts and seeds before cracking them open.

taste

Parrots experience a similar range of tastes as we do, though they seem to have no sensitivity to hot peppers! Most of their taste buds are not on the tongue but the roof of the mouth and, the tongue transfers minute food samples here to be tested before eating. A parrot's feet are very sensitive to touch, particularly vibrations. This allows them be aware of anything which might be crawling along their branch or perch at night when vision is very limited. The bird is aware of which side of their branch the disturbance is coming from and can take evasive action if needed. Parrots do not seem to have a good sense of smell.

The tongue is used first to feel for the weakest point in a nut. Then the beak is used to split it at this point. The tongue then checks the condition of the nut kernel.

⇩ *Parrots will choose high fat foods, such as sunflower seeds and nuts, whenever possible, so the supply of these should be rationed.*

Greys have a well-developed sense of taste. When tasting foods, parrots transfer minute quantities of food to the taste buds on the roof of their mouth. They can tell whether the food is high in fat or sugars very rapidly.

Breathing and blood circulation

Oxygen in fresh air is used to burn the bird's fuel, which is the food it has broken down. This fuel is used for bodily functions, such as keeping warm and powering the muscles for the bird's range of activities including flight. Flight is extremely demanding in terms of energy use. As a result, birds have evolved an elaborate breathing system that ensures oxygen is taken up at the elevated rates needed to support such levels of activity. The waste products of this activity are mainly carbon dioxide and water, and these are eliminated as the bird exhales with the same speed at which oxygen is used. In terms of effort, the difference between a bird walking and then flying is a bit like the difference between a car trundling around in first gear and then being driven at high speed in top gear. In addition to their lungs, which are similar to ours, birds have a system of air-sacs throughout their bodies. By shunting air around these air-sacs at high speed, birds can deliver a *constant* supply of fresh air to the lungs. The air travels over the lungs in the same direction all the time, rather than just being sucked in and blown out as with our breathing. These refinements mean a bird's breathing abilities are 25 percent more efficient than ours.

Parrots have a four-chambered heart similar to ours, and the bird's blood circulatory system works at a high-speed level to match its high-speed breathing. Even while at rest a parrot's heart beats at about 140 times per minute; more than twice the rate of a human heart. When flying, this increases to around 900 beats per minute, and this is quite normal for parrots. A grey's normal blood temperature is 104-106°F (40-41°C)—much higher than is found in humans. All these adaptations allow a parrot's body to operate at a much higher rate than is found in mammals of a similar size and this is needed to ensure the birds can fly well without becoming exhausted.

◁ *A resting or walking grey uses little energy compared to that used in flight. The initial take-off and upward flight demand a sudden surge in energy.*

Greys ⇨ *can make very rapid changes to their heart rate. The heart can beat more than six times faster than its resting rate within a few seconds.*

900

800

700

600

500

400

300

200

140

100

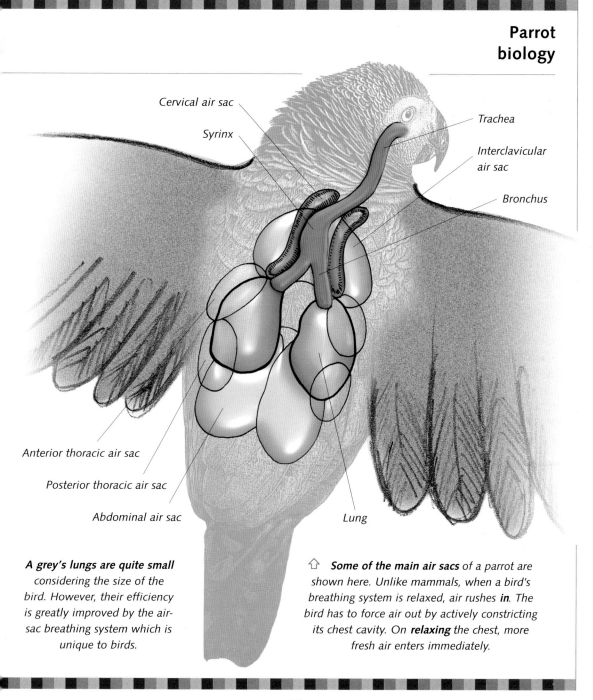

Cervical air sac

Syrinx

Trachea

Interclavicular air sac

Bronchus

Anterior thoracic air sac

Posterior thoracic air sac

Abdominal air sac

Lung

A grey's lungs are quite small considering the size of the bird. However, their efficiency is greatly improved by the air-sac breathing system which is unique to birds.

⇧ **Some of the main air sacs** of a parrot are shown here. Unlike mammals, when a bird's breathing system is relaxed, air rushes **in**. The bird has to force air out by actively constricting its chest cavity. On **relaxing** the chest, more fresh air enters immediately.

Vital systems: digestion

Wild grey parrots are vegetarians, eating a wide range of fruits, flowers, seeds, nuts, young leaves, and shoots. They have a preference for any food of a high nutritional value; this means they tend to favor foods with a high fat content, such as nuts and seeds, or a high sugar content, such as sweet, ripe fruits.

A grey's beak is a powerful, universal tool with sharp cutting edges which can be used with great skill. The beak is used in combination with the sensitive and muscular tongue to examine and manipulate items of food. Greys also use their feet in combination with the beak to hold larger items of food when necessary (most greys use their left foot). Unlike most other birds, parrots use their beak in a chewing action to chop up food their into small pieces before swallowing. They also discard parts of the food which are poor in nutrients, such as the skins of grapes by using the beak to peel this off.

Food is rapidly digested

The food then passes into the bird's crop. The crop is an extension of the esophagus, where food is stored before the next stages of digestion. It then passes to the proventriculus, a part of the bird's stomach where proper digestion begins as digestive juices are secreted and mixed with the food. Next, food passes to the gizzard.

This is a muscular part of the stomach where food is ground down under great pressure from the grinding action of this part of the gut. The inner surface of the gizzard is as rough as sandpaper and the physical crushing of food here renders it into a paste. The food then passes into the duodenum and the intestines where the well-digested nutrients are absorbed into the bloodstream. Indigestible items and waste products are voided via the cloaca. Parrots retain as much water as their bodies need, so they do not pass large quantities of watery urine. Instead, they

◁ **Using the foot as a hand,** greys can tackle a wide range of hard-shelled nuts quite easily.
⇩ **Parrots chew up their food** into suitably sized pieces with their beaks before swallowing it.

excrete uric acid as the white part of the droppings, again via the cloaca. A parrot's digestive system (its alimentary canal) is very short. This feature, combined with a bird's higher body temperatures, means food is easily digested within a few minutes. Some foods can pass right through a grey parrot in less than 30 minutes.

⇩ **This Timneh grey deftly removes** the skin of a grape and swallows the fruit pulp only.

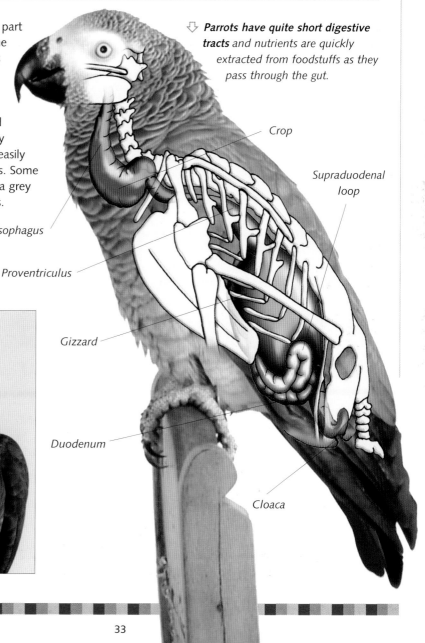

⇩ **Parrots have quite short digestive tracts** and nutrients are quickly extracted from foodstuffs as they pass through the gut.

Crop

Supraduodenal loop

Esophagus

Proventriculus

Gizzard

Duodenum

Cloaca

CHAPTER 4

How grey parrots fly

Greys are essentially flying creatures and they have evolved over millions of years to perfect their flying abilities. Flying for parrots is as natural as walking is for us. Flying birds never carry any "excess baggage." Practically every cell in their body is modified to reduce weight while retaining strength. They have very light hollow bones, very light feathers, and carry little or no fat. They also have a powerful engine; the massive pectoral muscles and large heart that enables flight to be sustained for hours if necessary.

It is the curved shape of the bird's wings which generate lift. As air flows over them, it results in the wings (and therefore the bird) being pushed upwards. The faster the air flows over the wing, the greater the amount of lift. The outer half of the bird's wing, the primary feathers, provide the propulsion needed to ensure this airflow is maintained. As the bird flaps downwards and backwards, air is pushed backwards over the wings. In addition to gravity, the main limiting factor in flight is the friction between the bird and the air, called "drag." How-ever, the bird's streamlined shape minimizes drag.

High speed flyers

There are several forms of flight. In powered flight, the wings beat regularly and the bird is able to climb easily and rapidly in the air. Greys fly at about 40mph (65kph) and can cover huge distances even if airborne for only a few minutes. This form of flapping flight is expensive in terms of energy use, but the bird's whole body is very well adapted to the needs of flying.

Greys also fly by gliding. Here, the bird does not flap, but keeps its wings held out as it moves forward. Since gliding is passive, it results in a loss of height as the bird moves forward. Eventually it either has to land, or switch its "engine" on and start flapping flight again to regain height. Greys can also hover, turn 360 degrees without flying forward, and deliberately stall at the point of landing as they put their feet out to grip the perch. The whole of the bird's body and wings are used for each flying task. While the primaries are used in propulsion, they are also used as air-brakes when a reverse thrust action is needed when landing.

⇧ *This bird is flying at a slow speed* and keeps his tail down to maintain control. Greys are highly manoeuvrable birds on the wing; they can also hover and spin around in a full circle.

Convex surface above wing

Low pressure

Air flow

Air flow

Air flow

Air flow

High pressure

LIFT   LIFT

Air flow

Concave surface below wing

⇦ **This bird is moving forward** *under powered flight and is half-way through the downstroke. The main thrust comes from the action of the primary feathers. The air flow over the wing generates lift.*

When coming in to land, *the bird* ⇨ *extends its feet forward and stalls in flight so that it stops moving forward at the point of landing, just as its feet touch the perch.*

⇩ **When stretching,** *parrots extend a leg and a wing from the same side of the body at the same time. The same side of the tail is also stretched as well.*

To facilitate landing, the wings are used as air-brakes.

Learning to fly

Greys normally leave the nest (fledge) at about 13 weeks of age, but they remain highly dependent on their parents for their food and safety for many more months. On first leaving the nest, the fledglings make their first attempts to fly. While the *urge* to fly is very strong in greys at this age, their *abilities* to fly are very poor. This is because the skills of flying have to be learned by each bird through simple trial and error experiences. Young birds will practise flapping while perched. This helps to strengthen their pectoral muscles (the main muscles used to fly) and gives them the feel of the power of their wings and the lift this generates. Soon they gain the confidence to take off for their first flight but usually they crash-land clumsily. However, after a few days their abilities to maneuver and control their speed and direction while airborne begin to improve and they soon land with more precision.

Young birds gotta fly!

In captive-bred greys it is vital to encourage these youngsters to fly at this stage. This ensures that the birds develop normally and that their muscles, including their heart, also develop as they should. If such young birds are denied the opportunities to learn to fly, they often remain unable to fly properly for the rest of their lives. This in itself can cause the birds behavioral problems as they are unable to escape from things which frighten them by flying away. Instead, they may become phobic birds with an exaggerated fear of harmless objects or actions.

Trial and error develops the skills

In the wild birds try to face into wind when taking off (just as aircraft do), since the faster the air moves over the wings, the more free lift the birds obtain. Captive birds rarely enjoy this advantage. It can take them longer to learn to fly well indoors where space tends to be very limited and there is no wind to help point them in the right direction when taking off and landing. However, after a few weeks, most captive-bred birds will have developed their flying techniques very well and become adept at using these skills.

⇩ ***Both young birds and adults*** *sometimes prepare themselves for flight by flexing their wings, often in a playful manner. When intending to fly to an unfamiliar place, the birds can take some time to make the final decision to take off.*

Grey parrots in flight

The small muscles within the wing are used to change its shape and the angle at which it meets the air. It is the massive pectoral muscles in the chest which give power to the wing during flapping flight. This arrangement of the muscles makes the bird's body very compact and keeps the center of gravity low.

Extensors

Flexi cardiulnaris

Pronator longus

Brachioradialis

Extensor carpi radialis

Triceps

Latissimus dorsi

Sartorius

Ilio tibialis

Ilio fibularis

Gastrocnemius

Crop

Biceps

Pectoralis

Peroneus

◁ **The propeller-like twist** in the primary feathers graphically reveals the thrust at play as this Timneh is half-way through his downstroke.

Safety in the home

The main areas to bear in mind regarding the safety of your bird are avoiding obvious household dangers and having your bird trained to accept some flight requests from you.

Windows and external doors should be kept closed *before* you ask your bird to come out of its cage. Alternatively, windows that have sturdy screens can be left open. In rooms where your bird is allowed to fly, any large windows should be covered with net curtains to prevent the bird thinking it can fly through the glass. Large mirrors can cause birds to fly into them, so it's best to remove these. Ceiling fans can cause a fearful reaction in some birds as the blades (even when not switched on) may be seen as a predator's wings, so these fans should not be present in any room in which a bird is either kept or allowed to fly. The kitchen presents many dangers to birds; these include hot surfaces, Teflon-coated pans, ovens, and electrical appliances, so it's best to avoid having birds here. Birds may also drown if they fall into a toilet or any other container holding water.

Careful introduction to a new room
When a bird is being encouraged to use an unfamiliar room where it will be allowed to fly, it will need to be introduced to the room properly. Without this introduction, the bird will not know which places are safe and suitable to land on.

This introduction procedure is a fairly formal training process whereby the bird is asked to step down onto those places where you would like him to go to and is then given a reward, perhaps a food treat, for doing so. Suitable places include chair backs, the sofa, window-ledges, table tops, and a stand for the bird (see page 46). After the bird has been introduced to these places as perches, he will be more confident about where to land and much less likely to crash-land when he does fly.

If your bird is ever suddenly

◁ **Large mirrors should be removed,** *reversed or covered up to prevent birds inadvertently flying into them.*

⇧ **If your bird crash-lands somewhere,** *avoid approaching him immediately, as you may startle him and so cause him to panic.*

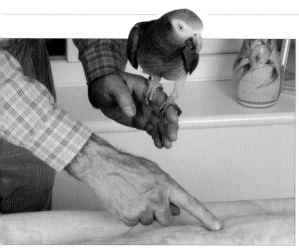

⇧ **It helps to reassure** a bird if you use your other hand to touch any new surface you are asking him to step onto, before setting him down there.

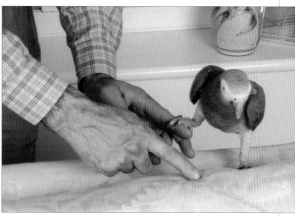

⇧ **Then set the bird down** using your usual verbal request for this and reward him with a food treat, toy or head scratch, whichever he likes most.

frightened of something and takes flight and crash-lands, do not approach him until a few moments have passed and he has collected his senses. If you approach a frightened bird too readily, he will associate you with the fearful incident and may become very afraid of you.

⇧ **Only once the bird is calm** and has collected himself after a crash landing should you approach him and ask him to step up onto your hand.

⇨
Flighted greys should be encouraged to fly for their physical and mental well-being.

CHAPTER 5

The cage

While it is almost a given that a companion parrot will be kept in a cage, the amount of time your bird spends in a cage each day will have a great effect on its quality of life and behavior. Greys need to spend many hours each day out of the cage, interacting with people and/or other birds just to remain mentally healthy.

The cage should large enough so that the bird can easily flap its wings while it is inside. So the main factor in deciding on the minimum cage size for your bird is the bird's wingspan; this is the measurement from wing-tip to wing-tip of the bird's wings when they are fully outstretched, as though the bird were in flight. African greys have a wingspan of 28in (71cm); the Timneh's is slightly smaller at 24in (61cm). A cage where measurements in all three dimensions (height, depth, and width) exceed the bird's wingspan will allow the bird to flap its wings. Sometimes it can be difficult to find a cage of these dimensions. However, so long as two of the measurements exceed this, and the third is, say, at least 24in (61cm), then the bird will be able to flap its wings. The *width* and *depth* of the cage are far more important considerations than its height since the bird will only use the top half of the cage anyway.

Cage construction

While the best and most expensive cages are made of stainless steel, most are made of mild steel which is then coated with various layers of paint. The paintwork is usually stove enamelled. This process hardens the paint and ensures it cannot be damaged or removed by the bird. The bars should be sufficiently thick and strong so that the bird cannot bend or damage them. Damaged bars can result in the protective coating being chipped away by the bird. Parrots enjoy being able to climb and this allows them some exercise. To aid this, the cage should have horizontal bars, as well as vertical ones. For the bird's safety, the spacing between the bars should be no more than 1in (25mm); this prevents the bird from poking its head out between the bars. It is a good idea to choose a cage with the food bowls mounted on swing-feeders which allows the food to be changed from outside the cage. The sliding tray in the base should be made of metal rather than plastic.

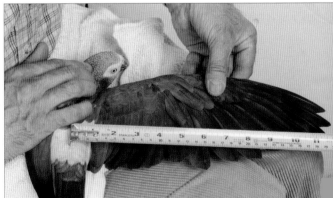

⇧ **To determine wingspan**, measure the distance from the center of the bird's back to the end of one outstretched wing, then double this figure.

⇩ **Within the cage** greys should be able to carry out most of their normal stretching and wing flapping actions, so ensure there is adequate space inside to allow this, while also leaving plenty of room for some hanging toys.

⇩ **A triple swing-feeder** fitted to the cage allows you to replenish the food bowls from outside the cage. This can be useful if you ask someone to care for your bird while you are out for the day.

⇧ **This cage is of sturdy construction** and has four swing feeders. The side bars are mainly horizontal which allows the bird to climb around easily. A flange near the base catches any spilled food.

Setting up the cage

Since almost all cages are made of wire on all sides, without a solid section, the cage should be positioned with its back against a wall. This will give the bird a greater feeling of security. If possible, position the cage so the bird can see out of a window, perhaps out onto your garden where the comings and goings of other birds will add some interest for your bird. However, do make sure the cage is never in full sun as the bird can very easily become overheated. The cage should be high enough so that the top perches allow the bird to be at your eye-level when you are standing next to the cage. If the bird is nervous, the height of the top perch should be increased, so that the bird can look down on you. If the cage has a grill just above its floor-tray, this should be removed as it prevents the bird from having access to the floor. The cage floor should be covered with newspaper sheets which are changed each day.

Fit different types of perches
To ensure the bird's feet are exercised properly, there should be a variety of perches in the cage and these should be of differing thickness. Usually, perches supplied with a new cage are of uniform and excessive thickness. Parrots have a locking mechanism in their feet when perched which allows them to grip the perch with little effort, but this does not work on thick perches. For a grey, the most comfortable (top) perch will be about ¾in (2cm) in diameter. This allows the bird to wrap its toes almost right around the perch. Other perches can be thicker or thinner. Perches made from any natural untreated

hardwood such as ash, hawthorn, maple, hazel, and willow are suitable.

Rope perches of natural fibers such as cotton, jute, or hemp are also beneficial. Softwood and plastic perches should be avoided. Most birds will chew their perches, and this helps them exercise their beak. With this in mind, perches should be seen as disposable items to be renewed frequently. Since they get dirty very easily, it is useful to have two sets of perches for each cage so you always have a spare set when needed. Sometimes an abrasive perch is used to keep a bird's claws less sharp. However, greys need fairly sharp claws to grip smooth surfaces properly. If you use an abrasive perch, this should be placed low down in the cage and not be the bird's favorite or top perch.

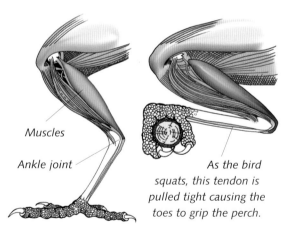

Muscles

Ankle joint

As the bird squats, this tendon is pulled tight causing the toes to grip the perch.

⇧ **When standing,** a bird uses more energy in its leg muscles. If a perch is too thick, the bird is forced 'stand' and cannot grip the perch passively.

A rope ring-perch allows a bird to swing or climb around on it.

⇧ **This perch is too thick** for a roosting or favorite perch as the bird cannot lock its toes around it; some birds fall off these thick perches in the night as their grip fails.

⇧ **Different perches provide different thicknesses** and textures for the bird's feet to use and this helps to exercise the foot and leg muscles. Flexible, semi-rigid perches can also induce the bird to play by swinging and climbing.

⇦ **This abrasive perch** has a twisted form and variable diameter which gives the bird a choice of different places to grip. It should be placed low down in the cage.

Furnishing the cage

The cage should be made as interesting as possible, so the way you furnish it is very important to your bird. Toys usually come in two different types: larger hanging toys and smaller foot toys. The hanging toys last longer than the foot toys, though they too will often eventually be destroyed by the bird as he chews them. You should be able to accommodate three hanging toys in the cage at a time. But to keep your bird interested and entertained, you should keep a collection of hanging toys and change one every few days, so the bird does not get bored. Foot toys are small enough for the bird to hold in one foot. These are often a bird's favorite toys, and they are usually designed to be destructible, rather than long-lasting. While you can buy foot toys in a shop, you can also make them for little or no cost. Suitable items include pine cones, small cardboard boxes, clothes pegs, lollipop sticks, pieces of twisted newspaper, small hardwood sticks, small hard plastic balls, and some puzzle toys. You can put food treats into the puzzle toys and your bird can be left to work out how to extract them.

Good quality toys and a roosting box
Toys must be safe for your bird, so avoid any with small or sharp metal parts that may be detached and swallowed by the bird. If toys have rings, the rule to bear in mind regarding their safety is that the rings should either be so small that the bird cannot get its head through them, *or* so large that the bird's whole body *can* pass easily through. If the bird becomes aggressive or overexcited when given a mirror, this should be removed from the cage.

All greys should be provided with a roosting box in the cage to gives them somewhere to hide away and to sleep in. Greys will also remain silent when in the box. The box should be made from ¾in (19mm) plywood. The internal dimensions should be about 12in (30cm) square by 7in (18cm) high. The box should be situated as high up in the cage as possible and be fitted securely. The entrance hole can be quite large; about 4in (10cm) square. Put some wood shavings and perhaps some chewable toys inside to keep the bird occupied when inside.

⬆ **This Timneh grey roosts** *in his cage-mounted box and also spends an hour or so each afternoon in here enjoying his siesta.*

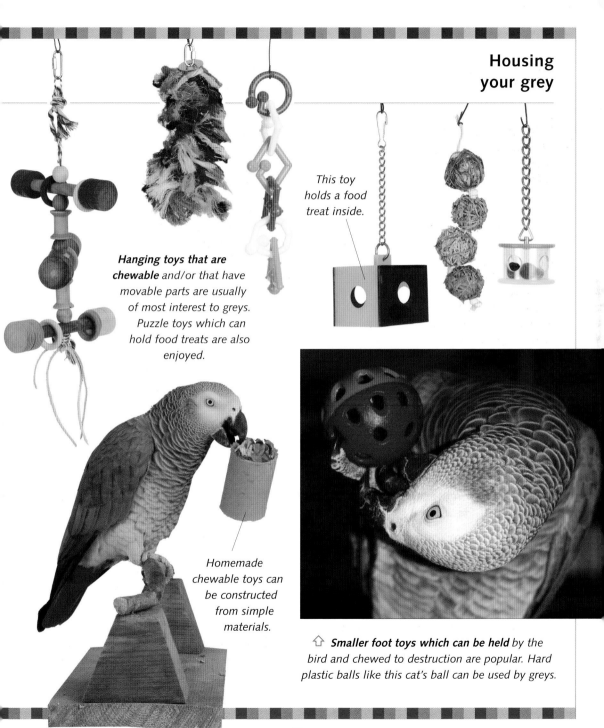

Hanging toys that are chewable and/or that have movable parts are usually of most interest to greys. Puzzle toys which can hold food treats are also enjoyed.

This toy holds a food treat inside.

Homemade chewable toys can be constructed from simple materials.

⇧ **Smaller foot toys which can be held** by the bird and chewed to destruction are popular. Hard plastic balls like this cat's ball can be used by greys.

Parrot stands and an aviary

While your bird is out of his cage, there should be several places that he can fly to and occupy. These might include chair backs, window ledges, tabletops etc. But your bird should also have at least one stand on which he can play with toys and eat some food while he is out. Stands come in a range of sizes, so get one with several different perches which can also hold food bowls and which has plenty of room for fitting toys onto it. In addition to these large stands, you can also obtain small, portable tabletop stands. You can carry these around with you from one room to another. As greys like to use a perch rather than having to stand on a flat surface, these are ideal. Most greys take to these stands very easily.

If you can provide your bird with an outdoor aviary, this is of great value to him. The aviary can be used as a day-flight, so you just put your bird out during the daytime when the weather is fine and bring him back in before dusk. The aviary can be used even in winter on fine mild days. Birds which have access to the outdoor world, have much better feather condition than indoor birds, so allowing your bird to experience some wind and even some rain from time to time will improve his feather condition.

Building a day-flight or aviary
To encourage flight the aviary should be at least 8ft (2.4m) long; the height should be at least 6ft (1.8m). If you build the back higher, you can have a sloping roof and this allows water to drain off. The aviary should be made from 1in (2.5cm) square 14 gauge best quality welded mesh. The auge is the thickness of the wire. You can use a wooden or metal frame. If a wooden frame is preferred, use 2in (5cm) or 3in (7.5cm) square timbers and hang the mesh on the *inside* as this gives some protection against the bird chewing the wood. Part of the aviary should be sheltered from rain and direct sun, so use some opaque rigid plastic sheeting for part of the roof.

The aviary floor can be made of concrete or gravel or left as natural grass. Furnish the aviary with plenty of perches, rope swings and toys and have swing-feeders fitted as well for your bird's feed.

⇦ *It's useful to have at least one or more stands for your bird to use. Large play stands with toys and food bowls attached enrich your bird's environment.*

A base-tray catches any droppings.

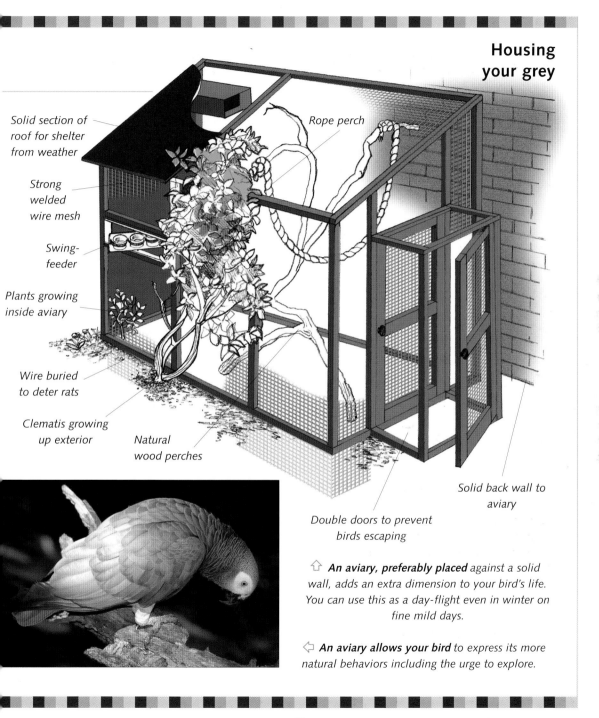

Solid section of roof for shelter from weather

Rope perch

Strong welded wire mesh

Swing-feeder

Plants growing inside aviary

Wire buried to deter rats

Clematis growing up exterior

Natural wood perches

Double doors to prevent birds escaping

Solid back wall to aviary

⇧ **An aviary, preferably placed** against a solid wall, adds an extra dimension to your bird's life. You can use this as a day-flight even in winter on fine mild days.

⇦ **An aviary allows your bird** to express its more natural behaviors including the urge to explore.

CHAPTER 6

Choosing nutritious foods

The usual parrot food found as a sunflower seed-based mixture is not suitable as the main diet for grey parrots. Such food is far too high in fat (it contains about 50 percent fat) and is seriously lacking in important vitamins and minerals. Many greys kept on such a diet will have chronic health problems due to vitamin and mineral deficiencies. This problem of poor diets for captive birds arises because greys are "programmed" to eat foods of the highest energy value which are foods high in fat. A wild grey needs a high fat diet as it will be flying hundreds of miles (km) every week and will burn off any excess calories. But a pet grey can never exercise at such a rate in your living room, so the diet for a captive bird needs to reflect that bird's real dietary needs.

Go for a 'natural' but varied diet
Food comprises carbohydrates, fat, and protein; the only other elements present are vitamins, minerals, and water. Grains, fresh fruits, and cereals are high in carbohydrates and these high-energy foods are used to keep the bird warm and as a fuel to power the bird's muscles. Nuts and many seeds are high in fats. Fat can be stored and broken down and used as fuel later. Legumes (peas and beans) and most cereals (rice, wheat, millet, etc.) are high in protein, which is needed to renew and replace body tissues including feathers. For pet parrots, the diet should be mainly carbohydrate (about 75-80 percent) with around 15 percent vegetable protein and only 5-8 percent fat.

In terms of nutrition, it does not matter how these foods are supplied. You could use pelleted foods formulated specifically for parrots, or alternatively a mixture of fresh natural ingredients. Most pelleted foods are certainly nutritionally well-balanced. However, parrots, like humans, appreciate a variety of textures and tastes in their food and since pellets are of uniform taste and texture, such a diet is lacking in stimulation for the bird. Greys have a range of techniques for dealing with the different, more natural foods they may encounter, so a diet based on fresh fruits, pulses, seeds, and grains adds interest for the bird. Some 'human' foods are either toxic or can cause a parrot to have

◁ *Given a choice of foods,* a bird will select those high in fat, but it's vital to ensure that your bird eats a **range** of foods each day.

⬆ *Most fresh fruits and vegetables contain good levels of vitamins.*

problems. Parrots should never be given chocolate, coffee, tea, alcohol, or avocado. Salty foods can cause kidney failure, so items such as chips and salted pretzels should be avoided.

Nutritional Values For Some Common Parrot Foods

	Fat	Protein	Carbohydrate
Apple*	0.1%	0.3%	11.5%
Cheese (Cheddar)	34%	25%	0.1%
(Caution: has very high salt content of 1.8%)			
Chickpeas*	5.4%	22%	50%
Maize (corn)*	1%	0.6%	84%
Mixed nuts	64%	16%	4.9%
Peanuts	46%	25%	12%
Pelleted foods*	14%	12%	60%
Pine nuts	69%	8%	11%
Bean mix*	1.4%	21%	45%
Rice*	1.2%	7.3%	77%
Sunflower seed	48%	12%	18.6%

* indicates the better, low-fat foods.

Note: Lost percentages to 100% are mainly composed of water

A healthy mixed diet

Since the nutritional needs of a parrot cannot be provided by a dry seed-based diet, and pelleted foods lack stimulation for your bird, it is suggested that you offer a mixture of legumes, fresh fruit and vegetables, and some seeds. The legumes have to be soaked and preferably sprouted in order for them to be edible. The seeds also have a higher nutritional value when soaked and sprouted. The following diet is therefore recommended for grey parrots.

   35 percent soaked/sprouted beans or bean mix (chickpeas, black-eyed peas, mung beans etc.)

   25 percent soaked/sprouted seeds and cereal grains (sunflower, safflower, hemp, millet, wheat, oats, rice, maize etc).

   40 percent fresh fruit and vegetables, such as apples, bananas, grapes, pomegranates, carrots, celery, sprouts, green/French beans, leafy greens, sweet potato, corn-on-the-cob, broccoli etc.

Preparing your bird's food

You might find it easiest to first mix your legumes (35 percent of food) and seed mixture (25 percent of food) together as a dry food and store it in this way. To prepare it, soak one day's amount of this in water for 12 hours. You can use *warm* but not hot water, as the heat would kill the mixture and prevent it from sprouting. The daily amount of food to be soaked will vary from one bird to another, but usually about 1 oz. (25-30g) of dry food will be enough (its weight will double after soaking). It is quite normal for the beans to smell during this process. After 12 hours you can feed the soaked mixture, but it is best to sprout and germinate the mixture following another 12 to 24 hours.

Getting the mix to germinate

To germinate the mixture, just keep the food moist at room temperature (not soaking in water) and rinse it thoroughly several times in cold water to prevent any bacterial contamination of the food. When you see a tiny white shoot appearing, the food is in the best condition to be given to your bird. Don't keep this food for more than one day after it is ready to eat; throw away all leftovers. Don't cook any bean/seed mixes, nor keep them in a refrigerator; just feed it raw.

In addition to this mixture, the bird should always have fresh fruit and vegetables *every day*.

⬆ *A mixture of seeds* before being soaked **(above left)**. *The same mixture after 12 hours of being soaked is shown* **(above right)**. *The same mixture after a further 24 hours, sprouted and ready* **(top)**.

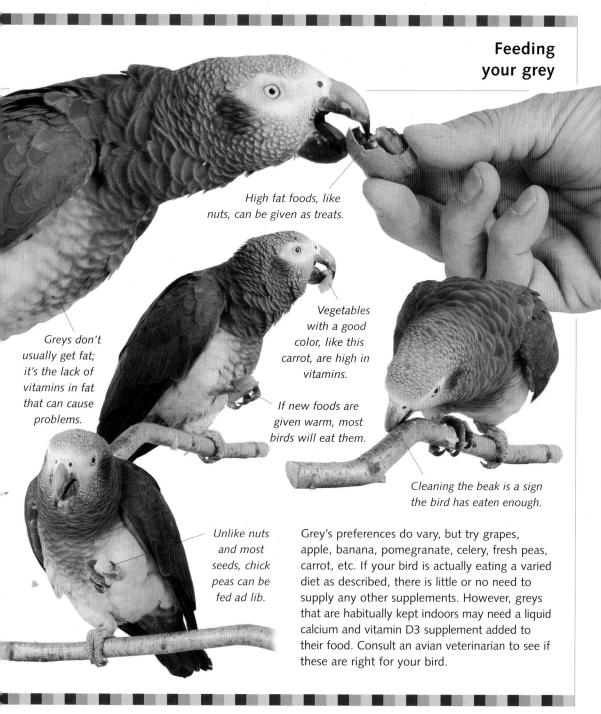

High fat foods, like nuts, can be given as treats.

Vegetables with a good color, like this carrot, are high in vitamins.

Greys don't usually get fat; it's the lack of vitamins in fat that can cause problems.

If new foods are given warm, most birds will eat them.

Cleaning the beak is a sign the bird has eaten enough.

Unlike nuts and most seeds, chick peas can be fed ad lib.

Grey's preferences do vary, but try grapes, apple, banana, pomegranate, celery, fresh peas, carrot, etc. If your bird is actually eating a varied diet as described, there is little or no need to supply any other supplements. However, greys that are habitually kept indoors may need a liquid calcium and vitamin D3 supplement added to their food. Consult an avian veterinarian to see if these are right for your bird.

CHAPTER 7

Understanding behavior

The main reasons for teaching your bird to accept a few training requests from you are much the same as those for training any animal you will be living with—you need to have good communication with your bird if it is to share your home as a companion animal. A trained grey who accepts a few simple requests from you makes a far better companion than a confused, untrained bird, who may either be nervous of people or aggressive towards them. Before you make a start on training, however, it is best to understand the motivation that lies behind behavior in general.

All behaviors are done for a good reason
The behaviors of any animal are always done for a reason. The reason is, essentially, that the animal knows it will get some benefit from performing the behavior. Birds will drink when thirsty and eat when hungry. They will tidy up their feathers by preening until they feel more comfortable. If something frightens a bird, it will try to fly away; when it likes something it will try to move towards it. In essence, your bird will perform a behavior because it desires the *results* of that behavior.

Using rewards
This awareness gives us an insight into how to work with a bird and teach it new behaviors. The key to success is

ensuring that you, as your bird's owner, always provide your bird with a *reward* for the behaviors you would like your bird to carry out. The reward is specific to your bird and can be anything which you know your bird *already* really likes—perhaps a small food treat, or having his head scratched, or a favorite toy to play with, or being taken to a favorite place on which to perch. This use of *reward-based training* is at the heart of a proper understanding of your bird's behavior. The study of behavior is called applied behavior analysis (ABA) and the use of methods based on ABA ensures a sympathetic cooperative method in working with your bird. ABA concentrates on *observable* behaviors; what your bird actually does and how frequently he does these things. While parrots will certainly have their own thoughts and feelings, ABA does not delve into this, since thoughts and feelings cannot be seen or measured in terms of their frequency or intensity.

⇧ *Tame and confident birds* often appreciate a head scratch and this can be a powerful reward.

Some greys have favorite toys and these can be offered as rewards when desired behaviors have been exhibited during training sessions.

Offer small toys and food rewards at or below beak level.

⇧ **Food treats,** can also work well as rewards.

⇦ **We cannot read the minds** of our companion birds. Good training depends on watching what your parrot **does**, not wondering what it **thinks**.

Training nervous birds

Grey parrots vary greatly in their degree of tameness and confidence. While most tend to be relatively nervous or shy, others can be very bold, even quite extroverted. Nervous greys require special care before and during training. Often, such nervousness is due to the way other people have handled the bird in the past and greys have very long memories. Some greys will be wild-caught birds which have been trapped and imported as pet birds. Wing-clipping sometimes causes nervousness and these birds may be extremely wary of people, particularly their hands. Nervousness may be made worse by the bird being trapped in a cage and so unable to escape fearful things happening near it.

Before attempting to ask a nervous bird to step up onto the hand, you will need to go through a gentle taming process which may take several weeks. The same principles of rewarding desired behaviors are used as in the more formal training sessions, but progress with nervous birds may be slow. These birds should always have a perch in their cage which is high enough to allow them to be above your eye level when you are standing by the cage. This will reduce the bird's fear of people who come close.

A careful, gentle approach for nervous birds
Start the taming process by sitting down below the bird while it is in its cage but not so close that it shows any signs of nervousness. Sit side-on to the bird and avoid looking directly at it. Let the bird see you doing something such as reading, or having a snack to eat. Keep these sessions quite short at first, just two or three minutes long, and extend them as the bird gets used to

⇧ **Step 1:** Eating your own food in front of a nervous bird can help to keep him calm.

⇧ **Step 2:** Later, if the bird seems interested in your food, offer him a tidbit through the cage bars.

Nervous birds hold their feathers down tightly.

you. Gradually sit closer to the bird so long as this does not make him nervous. After a few sessions the bird's confidence should improve and he may become interested in any food you may be eating. At this point, offer the bird a favourite tidbit through the bars of the cage.

At later sessions, try opening the cage door and offer a food treat directly to the bird while he is still in the cage. Just place your hand-held tidbit below his beak, provided he appears likely to accept this. Later, try leaving the cage door open and offer a treat after the bird has come out or just moved towards the open cage door. To get him to return, place a treat in his food bowl to tempt him back in. Always proceed at a pace which is comfortable for the bird. Use softly spoken words of encouragement as you make progress in this taming stage.

⇧ **This bird appears nervous** but inquisitive at the same time. Note the alert eye and how the head is stretched forward as he concentrates on something that has caught his attention. He has been badly wing-clipped which may contribute to his anxious demeanour.

⇧ **Step 3:** Next, encourage the bird to come to the open cage door, and then reward him with a treat.

⇧ **Step 4:** If he leaves the cage, encourage his return by conspicuously placing a treat in his bowl.

What companion parrots need to

So that your bird can spend as much time as possible out of the cage with you and your family, you'll need to teach him to accept a few simple requests or commands from you and other members of your household who wish to interact with him. Once trained to accept these requests, you will be able to ask your grey to fly to and from you, or leave certain places by using a verbal request. This allows you to have good control of your bird while he is out with you and means he will be reasonably easy to supervise. In most cases using reward-based training methods, a bird can be taught these requests in five to ten days. It is suggested you teach your bird the following requests in the order set out below.

STEP UP: This means step up onto my hand please. This is the first and perhaps most important request.

GO DOWN: This means please step off my hand onto another perch.

STAY: This means please do not come to me for the moment.

Assuming your bird can fly, make sure that you teach these next requests as well:

GO: This means fly off me and go to another place (perhaps the stand or the cage).

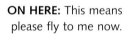

ON HERE: This means please fly to me now.

OFF THERE: This means please leave your present perch/place and fly to another place, but do not fly to me.

Where should you train your bird?

In most cases, you can train your grey in the same room as the cage. However, if your bird is aggressive around the cage, it may be easier to teach the first requests to step on and off your hand away from the cage or in another room. You'll need to have some way of getting your (untrained) bird to another room. In most cases, you can wheel the cage in to the other room, encourage the bird to leave the cage, then remove the cage before starting the training session. Nervous birds should always be taught in the same room as

⇧ **Birds should be asked**
*to leave any unsafe places
such as light fittings.*

Nervous birds *will learn* ⇨
*requests more easily if taught on
or near their cage.*

⇧ **A trained, trusting grey** *will learn to fly to you
on request—a special food treat offered as a
reward is the key to teaching this request.*

their cage. It is best to arrange
things so that the bird is asked to
step up and down from places
which are between waist and
chest height, so the back of a
chair is usually ideal. If this is
the first time the bird is to be
loose in the room, you should
remove any objects or ornaments
he may try to land on.

The first requests: stepping up

Since you'll be using reward-based training, you first need to know how you are going to reward your grey's good behavior during these sessions. You should find something which you know your particular bird already really likes as this provides the bird with the essential motivation for working with you. The reward may be a favorite food treat, or a particular toy, or having his head scratched. It's more effective to make sure that on training days the bird only gets these rewards by actually *earning* them: they should not be given for free, otherwise the bird has little incentive to co-operate. Most training sessions should only last for two to four minutes.

thumb down out of the way. You can touch the bird just above his feet with this hand as you say "step up." Repeat your request if needed and make sure the bird can see the reward being offered. When he does step up, praise him enthusiastically, then after only a second or two, say "go down," place him back on the chair back and give him his reward, with more verbal praise. Allow your bird plenty of time to appreciate the reward. Repeat this once or twice more, then end the training session.

It's best just to have one training session on the first day and try to end this on a good point, even if the bird has only stepped up once and had his reward. On subsequent days you could have two or three sessions, but try to work with your bird when you know that he is in a good, calm, and receptive mood. Whatever the bird does during these sessions, make sure that you remain completely calm and appear confident. A calm, atmosphere will greatly assist your bird in learning the requests. Soon he should be stepping up and down more easily as he gets used to these sessions.

Ensure your bird sees the reward
Start by having your grey perched on the back of a chair and make sure he is calm but attentive. If the reward is a toy or food treat, you can show him this as you hold it in one hand. Say your bird's name and try to make eye-contact, then approach him and place your other hand just above his feet and say "step up." Your step up hand should be held with your four fingers in line and your

◁ **Keep your thumb down** out of the way when letting a bird perch on your hand.

▷ **Testing to confirm a favorite** food treat. The bird selects from several items on offer to see which he prefers; that item can be your reward.

and going down

⇧ **Step 1:** To teach the step up, hold your reward in one hand and approach the bird with your other hand just above his feet.

⇧ **Step 2:** Give your verbal request to step up and touch the bird just above his feet with your step-up hand. Keep the reward visible.

⇧ **Step 3:** Praise the bird when he has stepped up, and give him the reward. A few seconds later ask him to go down.

⇧ **Step 1:** For the go down, turn the bird so he faces the perch from which he stepped up, with his feet just below this perch.

⇧ **Step 2:** Say "go down," hold the reward at a tempting height in front of the bird, and wait for him to step off you and onto the perch.

⇧ **Step 3:** Praise the bird when he has completed the move, give him his reward and move back a bit as he appreciates it.

Training *Stay* and *Go*

The *stay* request does not mean that a bird should stay exactly where it is, but is simply used to ask a bird to refrain from coming to you for the moment, perhaps when you need to leave the room without the bird following you. If the bird is approaching you and you do not wish him to step onto you or fly to you, just hold your hand with the palm facing the bird and say "Stay." If the bird stops, praise and reward him. If he still tries to come to you, use your hand in this same gesture to block his approach, whether he is walking to you or flying to you. A flying bird will soon learn to turn around and land elsewhere. When he does land, praise and reward him as usual. This *stay* request is very useful when other people are nervous of interacting with a bird. If other people (perhaps visitors) do not wish to interact with the bird, make sure that they know how to use this *stay* request to stop the bird from approaching them.

Teaching *Go*

This request is used to ask a bird to leave you by flying from you. Initially, teach this request by standing with the bird perched on your hand, about 3-4ft (a meter) from its cage or any other place he is already used to perching on. Have a reward for the bird conspicuously in view at the place you will be asking him to fly to. Turn your hand at the wrist so the bird is facing *away from you and towards the familiar perch and*

reward. At the same time, use your other hand, held lower down, to point to the place you want the bird to fly to, then say "Go, go" and swing the hand with the bird on gently but decisively in the direction you'd like him to go. The bird should leave you and land on the perch/cage top. As soon as he does, *praise him as he takes his reward.* When he is happy to fly from this short distance, gradually increase the distance to the perch. Then, practise this request in other locations, until you can ask the bird to leave you wherever you happen to be. If after giving the *go* request, the bird flies off you but tries to land back on you, just use the *stay* request to prevent this.

⇧ **Steps 1 and 2:** *Note how the hand with the bird on is turned away at the wrist. Using your other hand held lower down, point in the direction that you are asking your bird to fly towards.*

⇧ **This gesture** asks a bird to refrain from coming to you.
The same gesture can be ⇨ used for a flying bird; the bird will turn and land elsewhere.

⇧ **Step 3:** Then say "Go, go" as you swing your hand with the bird on it gently towards the intended perch. Your parrot should take off and fly towards the desired perching place on the other side of the room.

⇧ **Step 4:** When he lands on the designated perch, give him plenty of verbal praise and make sure that he gets his well-deserved reward immediately.

Teaching *on here* and *off there*

On here is a recall request, asking your grey to fly to you. This is much easier if your bird is already flying to you spontaneously, but it can be taught after the above requests have been accepted. If your bird is already flying to you, you should start to associate this with a verbal cue. So, when your bird is about to fly to you, give your command of on here and praise and reward him when he lands. Failing this, you will need a powerful reward to ask your bird to fly to you, so make sure you have this first. Place the bird on a familiar perch and stand about 3-4ft (1m) from him with your arm held out. If you are using a food treat or small toy as a reward, hold this in your hand so the bird can see it clearly. Your outstretched arm should be a little higher than the perch your bird is on, as birds prefer to fly *up* (rather than down) when coming to you. Say your bird's name and then say "On here" a few times. As the bird comes, stay completely still until he has landed and allow him plenty of time to enjoy his reward. If the bird does not come after a few attempts, take a break to stop your bird becoming bored and try again later. Once your grey is flying from a short distance, gradually increase this at later sessions.

The *off there* request

This is generally used as a safety request where you ask your bird to leave some place to which he should not have access. So, if a bird ever lands on an unsafe place such as an electrical appliance or perhaps a curtain rail, you can use this request to ask him to leave.

In practice you cannot teach this request predictably. However, when your bird does land somewhere that is unsafe or unsuitable, just approach him and say "Off there" as you wave one or both hands at him in an unfamiliar gesture. A wafting motion is often quite effective. You can also wave some harmless object such as a handkerchief in front of the bird. When he leaves, make sure he does not try to land on you, but lands on an appropriate perch, such as his stand or cage, and praise him for his cooperation.

This Timneh grey loves peanuts, so this is his reward when flying to his trainer.

A waved cloth reinforces the off there request.

⇦ **When a bird lands** on an unsuitable place, just promptly but calmly ask him to leave that perch.

⇧ **When the bird leaves** and lands on a suitable place, praise him for his compliance.

Just before asking the bird to fly to you, try to get his attention by saying his name and showing your reward at the ready.

⇧ **When first teaching this request,** do not ask your bird to fly more than a few feet. You can work on increasing the distance in later sessions when the bird is more comfortable with landing on you.

Further training hints

Generally, it should not be necessary to restrain a bird against its will. However, there will be times when this may be needed. You may need to administer medication or take your bird to the vet or remove him quickly from some danger. Again, it is best to accustom the bird to what is needed in these situations.

There are two ways to restrain a bird safely. The first involves asking the bird to *go down* on your chest. To do this, have the bird perched on your hand as usual, but facing you and place your other hand over the bird's back as you say "Go down" and draw the bird to your chest while you withdraw the hand he was perched on. The bird will grip your clothing as he lets go of your hand. Praise the bird and reward him with a gentle head scratch using your free hand. You can then carry the bird in this way as you leave the area and put him down elsewhere, saying "Go down" as you release him. It's useful to practice this request and to set the bird down on various familiar places before using this method to return a bird to its cage. In this way the bird will not associate it with having to go back to the cage, and this will make such a request easier to use when you may need to put the bird in the cage without delay.

A careful introduction to towelling

The second method involves the use of a towel, but this should not be confused with the practice of *forcibly* wrapping a bird up in a towel to train or tame it. Such enforced towelling is not appropriate at all. However, it is useful to get your bird used to being held gently in a towel

and this makes it easier for birds to be checked by a vet. Once the bird is trained in the requests as explained earlier, you can practice holding him in a towel. Use a towel of a bland or neutral colour, such as white or cream, as dark or boldly coloured towels may frighten your bird. Gradually introduce the bird to the towel by having the bird on your lap and offer him the corner of the towel to play with or to chew on. After a few sessions like this, let more of the towel come into contact with the bird's body. Eventually you should be able to accustom the bird to being held gently in the towel where you can restrain him for a few brief minutes. Reward the bird and encourage him at all times by giving praise, head scratches, or some other reward he already really likes.

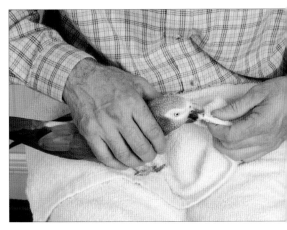

⇧ **Asking a bird to accept towelling** should be done over several sessions and at a pace which is comfortable for your bird. It should not be rushed. Use slow, careful movements and reward often.

   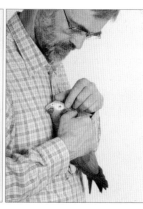

⬆ **This Timneh grey is asked to go down** onto the chest. Make sure the bird is facing you at chest height, then place your free hand over his back.

⬆ **Draw the bird towards your chest** so he touches you, then remove the perch hand so he grips your clothing with his feet. You can then reward him.

⬆ **After a few sessions,** the bird should allow you to let more of the towel come into contact with his body, and he may like to continue to chew on the towel during these sessions.

⬆ **The first time you are able** to wrap him up, reward him with a head scratch but keep this first wrap very brief, literally just a few seconds. Then release the bird, and again praise and reward him.

CHAPTER 8

Some frequently asked questions

This section looks at some frequently-asked questions about parrot care.

Should I get another (second) bird?

This question is usually asked for two reasons. Either the first bird has bonded to only one person in the family and other family members would like a bird which can be "their bird." Or the bird's main caregiver does not have the same amount of time to spend with the first bird as previously, and considers getting another one as company for the first bird. The matter of acquiring a second bird should not be gone into lightly. There are many issues to consider before doing this. What sort of bird would you get: the same species or a different one? What age should your second bird be, an immature one or an adult? Will the second bird just pair up with your first bird? If it does, will it want anything to do with you or anyone else, or will it reject human companionship? Will it even become aggressive to you or others if it pairs up with the other bird?

Trying to predict the outcomes of these issues is very difficult but some things are more predictable than others. Where you have two adult birds of the same species and opposite sex, they are very likely to pair up. This means they may prefer each other's company to yours. One or both of them may become aggressive to people if they perceive humans are interfering with their relationship with each other. When a second bird is not closely related to the first, this is much less likely to happen. Here the birds may become friendly towards each other without pairing up fully and this result is ideal. However, these are not predictable outcomes.

So, if you do decide to get a second bird and want to ensure that both birds appreciate human company as companion animals, you might be better advised to get a species which is not closely related to your first bird. Other species which originate from Africa, such as the Senegal, Meyer's or Jardine's parrot, could be tried with a grey parrot. To further reduce the chances of birds pairing up with each other, each should be housed in its own large cage but with the cages in the same room.

◁ **These two greys,** an African on the left and a Timneh on the right, not only get on well with each other, but they also both enjoy the company of people.

Both of these birds, a ▷ Timneh grey and a Meyer's parrot, are hand reared and each is bonded to a person. They sometimes show aggression to one another when they are overexcited.

Talking and the use of harnesses

When will my bird start to talk?

A grey's inclination to reproduce human speech can depend on the bird's age and whether it is kept with other birds. Lone birds are more likely to reproduce human speech. The value of talking will depend on the method you use to teach speech. While many greys will certainly mimic human speech without understanding the context, this seems a somewhat demeaning use of such an intelligent bird's abilities. If a bird is taught to use speech

⇦ *You can easily be fooled that your phone is ringing by your bird imitating the sound.*

in context, then your grey may well learn to associate spoken words with the objects and events in question. Here the bird is taught to use speech in much the same way you would encourage a human baby to start to learn to talk. So, repeating a word or phrase clearly, in association with events or with objects that are shown to the bird, will often result in the bird using these words in their proper context.

Some greys do learn to talk (mimic) within their first few months of life and most pet greys do talk within two years of age. But some greys never talk at all. There does not seem to be any difference between the talking abilities of Timneh greys and African greys.

Can I use a harness so that I can safely take my bird outdoors?

No type of leg restraint should be used on a parrot, as this can cause the leg to be dislocated. Although most greys dislike anything touching their feathers, some will accept a harness which can be used, with care, to take your bird outdoors. The harness is fitted around the bird's body and has a strap below for you to hold on to. There are several different types of harnesses. The better ones have an elasticated leash. This prevents a bird from being jolted suddenly if it tries to take flight and reaches the end of the leash. Birds will need to be properly trained, with care, if they are to accept a harness. Introduce the harness very gradually. On the first few occasions, make sure the bird only wears the harness for a *few seconds* and do this in a familiar indoor location. If the bird seems comfortable with this, gradually increase the time the bird wears the harness at each session. If at any stage the bird does not seem comfortable with the harness *do not persist with forcing this on a bird.* Instead, consider building a day-flight.

Associating a word ⇨ *with a specific object increases the chance of the bird using it correctly.*

◁ *Fitting a harness is not always easy, either for you or the bird. You should proceed slowly and carefully so the bird remains calm.*

⇩ *Greys have an ability to reproduce speech very accurately, including the tone and accent of the speaker.*

Various harnesses are ⇨ *sold but take care if you try to fit one of these on your bird. Most greys do not accept wearing a harness as they find them uncomfortable.*

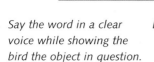

Say the word in a clear voice while showing the bird the object in question.

Beware of unwanted sounds copied at high volume!

Wing clipping

Should my grey have its wings clipped?

Wing-clipping is done in various ways and some types of clip are more severe than others. Clipping involves shortening some or all of the bird's main flight feathers (the 10 primary feathers). This may be done to one wing only, in order to deliberately unbalance the bird if it should attempt to fly; this is the most dangerous type of clip. Other forms of clipping where both wings are clipped evenly but lightly with some of the primaries left intact are less crude and allow the bird at least to fly down and land safely indoors. Although the molting process should eventually see a regrowth of any clipped feathers, this process can be problematic for clipped birds as they may break the new 'blood' feathers that grow down.

The commonest reasons giving for clipping a bird are to control its movements or for the bird's safety. However, *all* birds, whether clipped or not, are subject to some risks: clipped birds are just at risk in different situations. Where clipped birds escape from the home, there is more chance of them being caught by a dog or cat or of being run over by a vehicle. However, there is no chance of the bird flying off. Other problems for clipped birds can be more serious. When clipping prevents upward flight, some birds often become very fearful or phobic and generally have greatly reduced confidence.

A grey's most valuable means of escaping from a fearful situation is, of course, simply to fly away, preferably to a higher perch. Again, clipping denies the bird this most vital escape mechanism. Because the author prefers to keep his bird without having to clip its wings, the training section in this book explains how you can teach your bird some simple requests or commands from you to control its flight. This usually only takes a few days and these requests, once taught, give you all the control you need. Also your bird can behave more naturally by being able to fly.

If you do decide to clip your grey's wings, do so only after he has learned how to fly. Parrots that are clipped before learning to fly seem to be more prone to behavioral problems than those that learn to fly first. Also, remember that your bird cannot fly out of danger, so you will have to be extra vigilant about his safety.

⇩ *A 'mild' clip like this,* on both wings, can prevent some accidents.

⇧ **This bird's exposed tail** shows it has been clipped on both of its wings.

This bird is not clipped; the primaries extend to the same length as the tail.

Keeping an unclipped bird safe

What safety precautions should I observe with an unclipped bird?

When keeping birds which have not been wing-clipped it is important to follow some common-sense precautions.

Your bird should be properly supervised at all times when it is out of its cage and make sure to teach the bird the flight requests explained earlier in the training section.

Be aware of common household dangers. Birds should not be in rooms which have ceiling fans, open external doors and windows, or large mirrors. Large-pane windows can be very confusing for a bird so these should have curtains or net curtains hung in front of them. Do not allow your grey into the kitchen as there are far too many dangers here for birds like Teflon-coated pans, sources of intense heat, and toxic fumes.

Ensure your grey has several places outside the cage which it can use as perches. You may find it easier to manage the bird if these places are no higher than your head—for example, the backs of chairs and sofas, window ledges, and tables. Greys should not just be left to get on with things on their own in any new situation. As highly social creatures, these birds need guidance and encouragement from you. So, when introducing a bird to any new place or new room make sure to show the bird the places you would like him to use as perches. Just ask him to "Go down" onto these places using the requests that you have already taught him and reward him on the first few occasions with a tidbit or a favourite small toy to play with. When the bird is used to these places, he will be more confident about knowing where he can land when he does fly. Later, try using the *go* command to ask the bird to fly to these places from your hand.

While it is acceptable for the bird to *land* on your shoulder, the shoulder should not be seen as a normal perch. Always transfer the bird from your shoulder to your hand as soon as he lands there. Just use the *step up* command for this. Your *hand* should be the bird's normal perch when it is on you, not your arm or your shoulder.

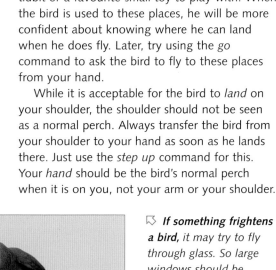

▷ *If something frightens a bird, it may try to fly through glass. So large windows should be screened with a blind or net curtains.*

◁ *Do not leave a bird on a new place for long; ask him to step back up after a few seconds.*

⬆ **It helps if you show** a bird places in a new room on which he is allowed to perch.

Don't leave a bird on your shoulder.

Ask him to step up onto your hand as usual.

Good hygiene

Can I toilet train my bird?

It is certainly possible to ask your bird to use certain places to do his droppings but this needs to be done with care. You will soon realise by watching your bird's body language when he needs to go to the toilet. Typically greys squat and wriggle their tails, just before passing droppings. At this point, you can try moving him to one of the places you would like him to use. Then praise him just after he has passed his droppings. It is important to have several places which your bird can use, otherwise he may become obsessed with only going to one place and this can cause him problems. After a few times of moving him to these places at the right moment, the bird should get used to this routine and then even make his own way there without your help. Alternatively, you can lay some paper beneath the places on which the bird perches to catch the droppings or just clean up immediately using a tissue and a good household cleaning product.

⇧ *Greys can be very messy feeders, so you'll need to clean the cage bars frequently on both sides of the cage.*

⇦ *Natural, hardwood branches used as perches soon get dirty so they need frequent cleaning.*

⇦ *Greys tend to pass droppings every 15 minutes or so.*

How often should the cage be cleaned?

It's best to use old newspapers for covering the cage floor and these should be changed every day. Once a week the whole cage, including the perches, should be scrubbed clean using a mild, diluted disinfectant and hot water. Some bird supplement suppliers sell 'bird-safe' disinfectant although other disinfectants are usually safe when diluted. Follow the manufacturer's recommendations regarding the strength of the solution it is advisable to use. Where a roosting box is used, birds rarely soil this, but the box should be cleaned thoroughly like the cage, once a week. The wood shavings or newspaper lining the box should be replaced once a week.

⇧ *Wood shavings, shredded paper* *or sheets of newspaper can be used to line the roosting box. Usually you will need to replace this once a week.*

How often should food bowls be cleaned?

These should be washed thoroughly at least once every day in hot water and mild detergent and then rinsed in plain cold water before refilling with food and water. Again bird supplement suppliers sell bird-safe antiseptic which you may wish to use as well when washing the food bowls each day.

⇦ *Greys on a healthy diet which includes fresh fruit and vegetables will make more of a mess of their bowls, so daily cleaning is essential.*

What about general health and hygiene matters?

With a common-sense approach, healthy birds pose few health problems for most people. However, care should be taken to avoid bird's droppings contaminating anywhere where human food might be prepared; so it's best to prevent birds having access to these areas, particularly in households with young children or elderly people, whose immune systems may not be as strong as other people's. In rare cases a disease called psittacosis may be transmitted to humans through inhalation of dust contaminated with infected particles in droppings. If you are ever ill and need to visit your doctor, always state that you keep birds in case this is relevant. If you think your bird is actually passing psittacosis in its droppings then the bird needs to be seen by a vet immediately for treatment. Fortunately psittacosis is rarely seen in humans but a far more common problem is people's allergy to feather dust, particularly from greys.

Remember to wash your hands before preparing your bird's food. Birds are sensitive to many common household chemicals so make sure your hands are clean before handling any food or the bird. Some people allow their birds to take a food treat from their own mouths, but this can result in birds being infected with bacteria which are naturally present in our mouths, so this practice should be avoided.

⇧ *Make sure your hands* *are clean before interacting with your bird or starting to prepare its food.*

Beak trimming, vacation care,

Do I need to trim my bird's beak?

It is not recommended that you ever try to trim your bird's beak. Greys need their beaks to be sharp just to deal with the range of foods they eat. The beak will only need to receive some attention if it is genuinely overgrown and causing the bird some difficulty in eating. Even then, treatment should only be undertaken by a specialist avian vet who is experienced in the care of parrots.

What should I do when I go on vacation?

If you have recently acquired a young bird, the bird will be very dependent on you, so you should simply *not go away at all* until the bird is more than a year old. To a very young bird, the sudden departure of the person to whom it is bonded can be extremely stressful. Under such circumstances, the bird may start to pluck out its own feathers. In the wild, a grey's parents would never desert the young bird and immature birds have no behavioral adaptation to cope with such a loss. With older birds, it is best to ensure they are used to the person who is going to care for them while you are away. The vacation sitter should be familiar with the bird's needs and be able to handle the bird in a similar way to you. Provided the birdsitter allows the bird out of the cage for several hours each day and the bird

relates at least reasonably well to him or her, and that other aspects of its care (such as food and caging) remain the same, the bird should cope well with your temporary absence.

Is it normal for greys to produce so much feather dust?

All grey parrots produce a lot of fine almost white powder from their feathers and this is quite normal. Most of it comes from the break up of soft down feathers on an area on the back, just above the tail. The bird often rubs its head here before preening and this ensures the powder is spread throughout the rest of its feathers. This ensures that the bird's feathers are kept water-proof and in good condition. It is necessary to spray your bird—preferably every other day—with plain water from a plant sprayer kept specifically for this purpose. You can buy a sprayer from any garden center; set the nozzle to produce a fine mist-like spray. Spray the bird in the morning so that it is dry before nighttime.

⇧ **Spraying your grey** with clean water every other day will help to maintain good feather condition.

Greys produce a waterproofing powder down ⇨ from feathers on the lower back. By rubbing their heads here, then preening elsewhere, they spread this down throughout their feathers.

and dealing with dust

Do I need to trim my bird's claws?

It is important to remember that greys need fairly sharp claws in order to grip smooth perches properly. When a bird has blunt claws, it is liable to slip off some perches or even fall and crash-land. So, in most cases, it is not necessary to trim a bird's claws regularly, they will only need checking occasionally and trimming if really overgrown. In the wild, a grey's claws wear down, and they are naturally kept at the right length. In captivity, since the bird is much less active, some excessive growth may occur and cause the bird problems. You will then need to trim the claws, or have a bird vet trim them. Rather than using clippers for this, it is best to use a small file, a nail file or some fine abrasive material simply to file off any excess growth while a helper holds the bird carefully wrapped in a towel. Alternatively, you can also use an abrasive perch in your bird's cage, so your bird's claws get some wear each time he uses this perch. However, parrots should not be required to use an abrasive perch for long periods as this can cause them some discomfort. So the perch should not be a favorite or top perch, but one lower down in the cage, perhaps beside a food or water bowl.

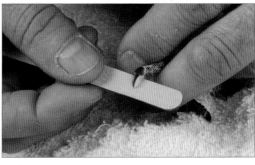

⇧ **When claws do have to be trimmed,** filing is safer than clipping, as there is little risk of inadvertently causing a bleeding claw.

CHAPTER 9

Submissive behaviors & biting

Growing up: from baby to adult

Parrots should never be blamed for whatever they do. It isn't helpful to project human emotions and values onto birds. All the behaviors that you see your bird performing are done because the bird is either trying to obtain something it needs or it is trying to avoid something that may be harmful to it. As a young grey begins to mature at two to three years old, the changes in its behavior are much the same as you would expect to see in any other animal, such as a puppy or a kitten, as it grows up. The cuddly-tame baby bird on sale at a breeder's premises or a pet shop will be a very different bird within two or three years and this is quite normal. As with other immature creatures, parrots adopt very submissive behaviors which encourage others to treat them gently while they are defenseless. However, as the bird matures, its needs change, so naturally does its behavior. To be prepared for your bird's generally more assertive, adult behaviors, just follow the training suggestions explained earlier, and accept the changes in your bird as it becomes an adult.

Biting

Most parrot people do get bitten from time to time and usually this is only a minor problem. However, *hard* biting which causes pain needs to be addressed carefully, otherwise you may unintentionally reinforce such biting and make matters worse. Biting often first occurs with birds as they begin to mature and the first incidents are commonly caused by the bird simply being overexcited, perhaps while in a playful mood. So remember to try to interact with your bird in ways that do not result in such overexcitement. If you are bitten hard, do *not* return the bird to its cage, otherwise you will soon have difficulty in doing even that! The most effective response is to simply turn your back on the bird, walk out of the room and close the door behind you. Stay out for two or three minutes. When you return, wait for the bird to

⇧ **If a bird bites you hard,** calmly leave the room without any reprimand, but make sure to close the door behind you so he cannot follow you.

interact with you, and carry on as normal. If biting occurs again, remain calm and repeat this tactic of leaving the bird alone for a few minutes. In most cases the bird soon makes the connection between biting and being left on its own and then it has an incentive to cease biting.

⇧ *It's important not to overreact* if you are suddenly bitten by your parrot.

⇦ *A young grey's typically submissive behaviours* do not last into adulthood. As normal adults, greys should show greater confidence and be more assertive.

Self-plucking

Preventing and curing self-plucking

Grey parrots are very prone to self-plucking. There is increasing evidence that self-plucking and other behavioral problems are due to conditions in captivity since wild parrots don't self-pluck. Causes of self-plucking may include the bird's diet or medical problems, so you should have your bird examined by a specialist avian vet if it starts to damage its own feathers. However, there is increasing evidence that it is the frustration of natural daily behaviors that appear to be the main cause of self-plucking. Greys most vulnerable to self-plucking are those whose living conditions include the following factors:

- They are solitary pet birds who are (or were) wing-clipped.
- They have been hand-reared.
- They spend long periods during the day in their cages rather than being out interacting with their owners or other birds.
- They have little or no opportunities to fly and, most importantly, no opportunities to forage for some of their food.

Wild greys spend many hours every day just finding and eating their food and they are programmed to carry out these foraging behaviours. But captive parrots have food available at all times in a bowl just a few inches away from them and are prone to severe boredom. It is the frustration of being unable to perform their foraging behaviors in captivity which causes so many behavioural problems.

To prevent and help cure self-plucking, you must try to keep the bird busy and occupied during the daytime. The bird should have a range of toys which it actually plays with and these should include toys in which food can be hidden. These are available as commercial puzzle toys and feeders from good pet stores, but you can also devise your own inexpensive versions. Try hiding some seeds in a cardboard tube filled with newspaper, or a tidbit inside a small box. Food hung up in small baskets or in bird-feeders used for wild birds can also be used. Giving your bird opportunities to fly, either indoors or in an aviary used as a day-flight will also help. Parrots need to have plenty of items which they can simply chew up to destruction. Most natural products are fine. Use cotton or hemp ropes, fresh branches from any fruit or nut trees, strips of rawhide leather, or even old phone books. The key thing is to keep your bird's beak and brain busy with other objects. With plenty of out-of-cage time and lots of things to chew up, your bird is much less likely to chew on its own feathers.

◁ *A food dispensing puzzle toy. Larger nuts can only be extracted from one of four holes: the bird has to learn how to do this by manipulating the toy to gain access from the right hole.*

Birds with
self-plucked
wings and tail
often have poor
balance.

⇧ *A foraging toy.*
This grey chews
through a thick
cardboard tube and
newspaper to get at
an almond nut
hidden inside.

⇧ *Self-plucking is
a symptom* of some
other problem and is
only seen in captive
birds. Wild greys do
not self-pluck.

⇦ *Plucking often
starts* in small, localised
areas. This grey has
started to pluck, but only
on his legs and belly. If
addressed early on,
plucking is easier to cure.

Nervousness and 'phobic' greys

Greys which cannot fly, perhaps because they are wing-clipped, are very susceptible to becoming phobic and showing an apparently exaggerated fear of certain actions, objects or people. When a grey is nervous or afraid, he may either remain quite silent or make a growling sound. He may also start to panic if the cause of the problem is not removed promptly. Sometimes, the fear is so great that the bird may thrash around in its cage. This behaviour has nothing to do with aggression; it means that the bird is really afraid of something. You should remove the source of your bird's fear *immediately*, even if the source is you! Just walk away, even leave the room, but do so immediately. Make sure that your bird has a perch in the cage which is above your eye-level. This helps to reduce the bird's fear of people who come close. Birds do not show any evidence of being comforted by reassurance as humans do, so if the bird is afraid of you or something you have done, attempts at reassurance are pointless and can even make a bad situation much worse.

If your bird crash-lands somewhere and the next thing that happens is you approaching him to reassure him, he may associate you with any pain he may be feeling at this point, and so begin to fear you as being linked to the cause of his pain. In this situation, remove yourself from the bird until he has collected his senses and has had time to calm down.

Great care is needed with fearful birds
Getting a bird to overcome its nervousness has to be conducted at a pace which is comfortable for the bird. See the section on nervous birds (pages 54-55) and follow the guidelines described there. Getting a bird to return to its former tame condition following some fearful event can take time. You'll need to be patient and work slowly and carefully with the bird, using whatever rewards you know that the bird is likely to accept. If other people can work with the bird better than you, then give them the opportunity to do so at first. You can then help later when the bird's confidence is showing signs of returning.

⇧ **Eating your own food** in front of a bird can help to get him to accept your presence calmly.

⇦ **Don't approach a frightened bird** until he has calmed down; your 'help' may cause the bird to feel more fear. Even your helping hands may seem frightening.

Though only a few weeks ⇨ **old**, this grey has been badly clipped. This may cause phobias in later life.

⇧ **If a bird crash-lands** somewhere, do not approach him until he has collected himself. Make sure that he has calmed down before asking him to step up onto your hand.

Destructive chewing and noise

As wild birds, greys are kept quite busy by chewing on wood, leaves, buds, and flowers as they search for food in the trees. Despite the fact that they usually have food available at all times, pet greys will still try to replicate this behaviour in the home environment and this is

⇧ ⇩ *Chew-toys can be fabricated from natural items, like pine cones above, or be bought from pet shops, like this straw chew ball below.*

⇧ **When not supervised,** *greys may chew woodwork, such as doors and items of furniture.*

quite normal. If the bird does not have access to suitable things to chew, he is very likely to start chewing anything he can get his beak into, including your furniture, doors, and ornaments.

So it is important to provide your bird with destructible toys to keep him busy. While you can certainly buy these from parrot stores, you can also make up your own. Try using clothes pins (remove the spring); pieces of hardwood such as oak, apple, cherry, hazel, etc.; cardboard; newspaper; pine cones; rawhide leather strips; or short lengths of cord made from natural fibers such as cotton, hemp, or jute. Also, providing your bird with opportunities to forage for some of his

favourite foods hidden in puzzle toys will help to divert him from chewing unsuitable objects. Again, you can get these toys from pet product suppliers or devise your own versions. Greys will soon learn to search out food treats hidden in pieces of crumpled newspaper inserted into cardboard tubes.

problems

This chew-toy is made ⇨ from natural fibres and is ideal for greys. Make sure that you introduce all new toys carefully—your bird should see you playing with them on several occasions before they are placed inside his cage.

⇦ *Toys with removable parts often interest a bird more than static, fixed toys.*

If greys are ⇨ allowed to hear loud noises or swearing repeatedly, they may start to mimic these sounds, so take care of what your bird hears.

Noise

Unlike most other parrots, greys are not usually noisy birds. However, if your bird does start to make a loud repetitive sound, this is usually because he needs attention and is bored. Birds that spend too long in their cages will be prone to this behavior, so they just need to be out more and be kept occupied. When a bird has plenty of time out of the cage but also starts to make a loud noise which causes a problem, it is vital that you do not inadvertently reward the bird by giving him any attention, even by saying "No" to him. Here, the most effective solution to such a noise problem is for you, and everyone else, simply to leave the room each time your bird starts to produce the unwanted noise. Eventually, most birds realize that their behavior has caused you to leave him. When he makes this connection he will have an incentive to stop making the unwanted noise.

CHAPTER 10

First aid & general health care

Your parrot should stay physically and mentally healthy provided it has a good diet, plenty of time each day out of the cage to fly and enjoy good exercise, and a stimulating environment with a good relationship with its carers. However, you should be prepared for the possibility of illness long before it occurs by making sure that a good specialist bird vet is available. It is important to use a vet who has considerable experience of treating birds, rather than an ordinary vet whose skills may not include avian medicine. It is also recommended that your bird should be examined at least once a year for a general health check-up. Most bird vets are members of the Association of Avian Vets and various websites list their contact details. Bird vets are also listed in avian publications each month. Good bird vets will have some or all of the following facilities:

- Anaesthesia by isofluorane gas (this is very safe anaesthetic for birds).
- Ability to do imping (restoring flight by repairing a bird's wings following any wing-clipping).
- Ability to do complete blood count and biochemistry tests.

- Availability of an endoscope for internal examinations and diagnosis.
- Ability to take tissue samples (biopsies) for testing and analysis.
  - Staff who know how to handle parrots correctly, using a towel (not gloves) to minimise stress.
  - 24-hour hospitalization facilities for birds.

Assessing the health of your bird
Healthy birds are active for most, but not all, of the daytime. They have bright, wide open eyes and no discharge from the nostrils. Breathing is silent. Healthy birds are alert and well aware of things going on around them. The body feathers should be relaxed and slightly smoothed down; neither puffed up nor held down with an excessive tightness. The bird should be eating normally and passing droppings normally, without undue straining. The area around the vent should not be soiled by the bird's droppings. When resting or sleeping, a healthy bird usually stands on one foot for much of the time. If your bird does not show these normal healthy signs, something may be wrong. Remember, sick birds will always try to hide signs of illness, so by the time a bird *appears* unwell, it is usually very ill indeed. Make sure to act without any delay in getting your bird treated if you ever think he may be unwell.

⇧ *A Timneh grey in excellent condition.* A clear, alert round eye, no discharge from nostrils, no frayed or damaged feathers.

◁ *A healthy bird* will spend quite a bit of time preening and keeping its feathers in good condition.

There are now some good ⇨ specialist bird vets whose knowledge of parrots is far better than vets who just concentrate on dogs and cats.

Caring for sick birds

Recognizing sick birds

Sick birds often appear tired with fluffed up feathers and sunken, dull, or half-closed eyes. They may have difficulty balancing or using a perch and may go to the floor of the cage instead. Sick birds often shows signs of being less aware of things going on around them. The droppings may not be normal and the bird may not be eating as usual. Sick birds often lose weight and this loss can be rapid. Make sure you know your bird's normal weight and check this from time to time.

Sick birds: what to do

If the bird can be weighed without causing further stress, then do so and write the reading down. Sick birds usually gain great benefit from simply being put somewhere very warm, 79 to 86°F (26 to 30°C) and kept out of bright lights. You can supply heat using a ceramic infrared heat lamp placed above the cage (this emits heat without any light). Place this so the bird can move away from the lamp if at any time it feels too hot. Use a thermometer to check the temperature around the cage (but keep this out of reach of the bird). The provision of heat will mean the bird will need to drink regularly, so make sure the bird has easy access to drinking water and wet foods such as grapes or apples. Once the bird is receiving heat treatment, phone your vet, explain the bird's symptoms, and get emergency advice without delay. When taking your bird to the vet, keep it very warm all the time. Stress alone can make things worse for the bird, so always act calmly. Restrict the bird's ability to see out of its carrier cage during travelling as this also helps to reduce stress.

Items for your bird's first aid needs:
- Avian vet's contact details.
- Cotton balls and cotton swabs—used to help stop bleeding.
- Styptic pencil (to stop bleeding of claws or damaged beak only).
- Antibiotic ointment.
- Avian antiseptic.
- Electrolyte solution, such as Pedialyte
- Avian multivitamin powder.
- Glucose powder.
- Towel—should be bland color such as white or cream. (Dark towels may frighten the bird.)
- Ceramic infrared heat lamp or hospital cage.
- Room thermometer.
- Small syringes and a bent spoon for giving medicine or food.
- Forceps.
- Pair of small sharp scissors.
- Hand feeding formula.
- Travelling cage with one low-level securely fitted perch.
- Good quality electric scales.

⇩ **Sick birds often appreciate extra heat.** The heat lamp over this cage allows a bird to move into and out of the heat at will.

⇧ **A small, simple cage** is best for transporting a bird. Keep it covered while the bird is in transit.

It's very useful to know ⇨ your bird's normal weight. You should also weigh him if he shows signs of being unwell. Note the weight and let your vet know.

CHAPTER 11

Searching for a lost bird

Most parrots escape through an open door or window. But if owners have got into the habit of letting their bird perch on their shoulder (instead of their hand), these birds commonly escape as the owner unwittingly walks outdoors and the bird flies off. It is best to prevent a bird from using your shoulder as a perch; instead, always have the bird on your hand. Grey parrots fly at about 40mph (64kph), and can be many miles away within a few minutes. In the event of an escape, what should you do?

⇦ *Countless "shoulder birds" escape. Keep your bird on your hand to prevent escape!*

You'll need a small ⇩ *travelling cage with a low perch to put your bird in once caught.*

First, you should have these items ready:
- A good pair of binoculars.
- Some of your bird's favorite food treats and the food bowl from his cage.
- A travelling case and/or cloth holding bag with drawstrings to put the bird in if and when you do catch him.

If a bird has panicked while escaping, it will probably fly a great distance before coming down to land in an exhausted state. However, a bird which escapes while it is otherwise quite calm usually does not go far. In this case the bird is most likely to fly in a wide circle around the point of release looking for somewhere near to home to land. Most parrots that find themselves flying outdoors will be confused simply because everything is unfamiliar to the bird. Greys do not like to land on a perch unless they are already familiar with it. Tree branches, which may be blowing in the wind, may be frighten the bird and bare rooftops or TV aerials may also not be acceptable. Eventually though the bird will land as it becomes exhausted.

Searching in the tops of the trees

Escaped birds often land in the *tallest* tree in the area and then try to hide by climbing down into the foliage. At this point the bird will be very tense and liable to fly again unless it is allowed to calm down. In winter, when most trees have lost their leaves, you may find the bird by direct searching, using your binoculars, but in summer it can be extremely difficult to spot a parrot in a leafy tree. In these circumstances, it's best to rely on your ears to start with. Listen out for your bird's calls. Tame pet birds (as opposed to aviary birds) will often respond to the familiar voice of their owner, so use your usual calls and whistles as you search for your bird.

What to do if a bird escapes?

◁ **Escaped birds often land** in the top of the tallest tree in the area and are then reluctant to come down.

⬇ **Parrots can survive in the wild** if they find food. This Timneh grey is enjoying rowan berries in a suburban garden.

How to recover escaped greys

The more people who know about your lost bird, the greater is your chance of someone spotting him and telling you. Make copies of a short note with a picture of your bird and details of when it was lost and post this to as many

⇧ **With a ladder** you will be able to climb up closer to your bird to encourage him to come down.

people as you can in your neighbourhood. Include all your contact details. When someone sees a strange bird, perhaps in their garden, they often contact the police, local radio station, local vets, or the ASPCA. So make sure you contact these organisations with details of your bird.

Stay calm and request a *step up*

When you find your bird, he is likely to be high up in a tree and will be nervous of flying down to you. The bird's instincts tell it to stay high up where it will feel safer. However, a bird will often actually try to *walk* down if you can devise a way of approaching him that offers him a route to you that doesn't require him to fly. Usually this means you'll have to use a ladder and make some attempt to go up towards your bird. Even being just a a few feet (1m) or so off the ground can be a great help in persuading the bird to come towards you for a food treat. At this point it is best to offer the bird a small tidbit and just stay with him as he eats this to keep him calm. Depending on how the bird is used to being handled, you will have to decide how you are going to secure him. Birds trained to accept the usual requests *will still obey these* even outdoors. So, if you have trained your bird, it is very likely to simply *step up* when asked, and walk onto your hand. If you are up a tree, you should have a bag or box into which you can put the bird before you climb down. You can make a suitable bag from a small pillowcase. This should have a drawstring and a strap which goes over your shoulder to leave your hands free when coming down the ladder. Or you can lower the bag down to the ground on a line.

If you find your bird, but are not able to catch him by nightfall, return to the same place *before light the next morning* and try again. In summer, this will mean getting there before 4am. Most parrots do not fly after dark, so he will almost certainly still be there.

⇩ *A carrying bag with
drawstrings is ideal for holding
your bird in as you climb down
from a
tree.*

⇩ *A good pair of binoculars
are invaluable when you are
searching for your lost bird,
particularly when the
trees are in leaf.*

⇧ *Escaped birds are
nervous of flying
down from a tree.
If you can move up
towards him a bit, he is
more likely to climb down.*

Index

Note: Page numbers set in *italic* type refer to captions to pictures; page numbers set in **bold** type indicate the main subject reference.

Picture Credits

Published by
Interpet Publishing,
Vincent Lane,
Dorking,
Surrey RH4 3YX,
England

© 2007 **Interpet Publishing Ltd.**
All rights reserved

ISBN 978 1 84286 168 4

Editor: **Philip de Ste. Croix**
Designer: **Philip Clucas MCDS**
Photographer: **Neil Sutherland**
Diagram artwork: **Martin Reed**
Index: **Amanda O'Neill**
Production management:
Consortium, Suffolk
Print production: **Sino Publishing
House Ltd, Hong Kong**

Disclaimer

Unless otherwise credited below, all
the photographs that appear in this
book were taken by **Neil Sutherland**
especially for Interpet Publishing. The
publisher would also like to thank
Mike Taylor at **Northern Parrots**
(www.24Parrot.com) for kindly
supplying the pictures of cages and
cage furnishings that are credited
below.

**Frank Lane Picture Agency/flpa-
images.co.uk**: 7 right (Jurgen and
Christine Sohns), 11 bottom right
(Gerry Ellis), 16 (Angela Hampton),
89 top (Angela Hampton).

Greg Glendell: 15 top left, 91 top
left, 91 bottom.

iStockphoto.com:
Terry J. Alcorn: 28 left.
Mark Atkins: 9 top right.
Lee Feldstein: 71 top left, 83 bottom.
Steffen Foerster: 3 right, 9 left, 11 top.
Yves Grau: 9 bottom right.
Aleksejs Jevsejenko: 21 top.
Jill Lang: 15 top right, 22.
Chris Mampe: 7 bottom left, 25 top
right.
Jurie Maree: 93 top left.
Ralph Martens: 43 top right.
Nancy Nehring: 13 top right, 27 top
right.

NiseriN: 92.
Nuno Silva: 82 (background hand).
Willie B. Thomas: 87 bottom right.
Stefan Witas: 93 bottom right.

Lars Lepperhoff: 8.

Northern Parrots: 41 left, 41 bottom
right, 46, 85 top, 85 centre.

Professor Irene Pepperberg: 3 inset
bottom left, 20 top left.

Shutterstock Inc.:
AJE: 57 top left.
Palis Michael: 13 bottom right.
Jill Lang: 18 bottom right, 23 top, 45
bottom right, 55 top right, 79
bottom left.
Lana Langlois: 17 top left, 32 top
left.
Carrieanne Larmore: 43 top left.
Jasenka Luksa: 49 top.
Suponev Vladimir Mihajlovich: 27
bottom left.
Michelle D. Milliman: 53 bottom left,
69 bottom right, 85 bottom right.
Tom Royal IV: 47 bottom.
Brian Upton: 15 top left, 79 bottom
right.

Sonny Stollenmaier: 14-15 (bottom
three images), 19 bottom left.